About the Authors

Zoë Desmond is a single mother to Billy and founder and CEO of Frolo, the award-winning app that supports and empowers single parents. Frolo has featured widely throughout the media, including in *Grazia*, *Sky News*, *Hello!*, the *Evening Standard*, the *Telegraph*, *The Irish Times*, won Social Media App of the Year at the UK APP Awards in 2021 and is a multi-time editor's favourite on the app store.

Rebecca Cox has been a single mother to her son Jack (7) for six years. A journalist with fifteen years' experience, her work covering women's rights, dating, fashion and lifestyle has been published by *Elle*, *Glamour*, *Country & Town House* and more. Her articles on single motherhood have featured in publications including the *Evening Standard*, *Grazia* and *Harper's Bazaar*.

How to be a HAPPY Single Parent

Rebecca Cox and
Zoë Desmond

PIATKUS

PIATKUS

First published in Great Britain in 2023 by Piatkus

1 3 5 7 9 10 8 6 4 2

A CIP catalogue record for this book
is available from the British Library.

ISBN: 978-0-349-43601-2

Typeset in Sabon by M Rules
Printed and bound in Great Britain by Clays Ltd, Elcograf S.p.A.

Papers used by Piatkus are from well-managed forests
and other responsible sources.

Piatkus
An imprint of
Little, Brown Book Group
Carmelite House
50 Victoria Embankment
London EC4Y 0DZ

An Hachette UK Company
www.hachette.co.uk

www.littlebrown.co.uk

Zoë: for Billy
Thank you for giving me the inspiration, courage
and strength to embark on this incredible journey.
I love you beyond words and I am so proud
to be your mum.

Rebecca: for Jack
This is, as you told me, your book. By loving you
with all my heart I've learnt how to love myself,
and finally and truly to be happy.
I love you more. (Possible.)

... and for anyone whose family doesn't look the way you
thought it would or should: it's beautiful, just as it is.

Contents

Choose Your Own Adventure –
an Introduction

Parenting is, arguably, the hardest job in the world. Whether you are full- or part-time, or perhaps you're just thinking about it, you are now, or soon will be, the entire parenting team: the CEO of your family, the solo monarch of your domain. Congratulations! This is single parenthood. Welcome to the village. These first days, weeks and even months of single parenthood can feel incredibly lonely, but we're here to tell you that you are not alone. In the UK, single parents account for almost 20 per cent of all families. There are 3 million single-parent families in total. In the US, it's 13 million. There is a whole world of single-parent friends out there, who are not only going to be your support network but they're also going to amaze and inspire you with their brilliance. And, although you don't know it yet, you're going to inspire them too.

'You always have to carry on. And you can, because
you have to.'

Kate Winslet on single parenting

This book is about carrying on. It's about going beyond carrying on and surpassing your wildest expectations of what you are capable of. Your family might not look the way that you've grown up being told that it should. Your family might not even look the way you thought single-parent families should look like. But your family *is* beautiful.

All about us

Zoë's story

I became a single parent when my son Billy was one, when my relationship with his dad had broken down. I felt like my whole world had fallen apart. I found myself not only still in the throes of navigating new motherhood but I was now navigating my new identity as a single parent too. I didn't know any other single parents at the time, so I felt like an alien in my new identity, and it came with feelings of shame and guilt that I couldn't provide the family unit that I had always dreamed of for myself and Billy. It was a challenging time and a grieving period, and putting one foot in front of the other was hard and lonely. I started wishing the weekends away, as seeing other people playing happy families compounded the feelings of loneliness and isolation I was having, but I put on a brave face for friends and family because I didn't want anyone to feel sorry for me, or for me to be a burden. I found myself longing to connect with other single parents, and I started imagining what it would be like to have other single parents who would also be free at the weekends for playdates, Sunday lunches and weekend adventures, and others who could relate to the ups and downs of the experience. I scoured the Internet and the app store for the single-parent community I was desperate to find, but much to my disappointment it wasn't there.

When I learnt that up to one in four families are single-parent families, I realised that single parents are everywhere, but I wondered how I could find the ones in my area. This is when I started to dream up a solution, an app that made it easy to discover and connect with like-minded single parents in my area, and beyond. In 2019 I launched the Frolo app (more on this in Chapter 8).

Launching Frolo has completely changed my life. I have benefitted from the app in the most profound ways, as has my son. I have made the most incredible close-knit friendships (including my dear friend, and the wonderful co-author of this book, Rebecca!), and now I have this beautiful extended frolo family, and I honestly don't know what I would do without my frolo friends and the support from the community in my life. They say that when life gives you a lemon, make lemonade, and my version of that was to turn what I thought was the worst thing that ever happened to me into the best thing that has ever happened to me. It makes me so happy to see that single parents everywhere using Frolo are benefitting in the same way too.

On becoming a single parent, I felt sad, depressed, overwhelmed and lonely. But now I feel proud, supported, empowered and so grateful for the many incredible experiences and people that I have been fortunate to bring into my life through being a single parent. I hope that whatever your situation is, and however you feel about the point you find yourself at right now in your single-parent journey, that you find in this book the guidance to give you reassurance and hope, because there is so much to be hopeful and excited about, I promise.

Rebecca's story

I got married to my university boyfriend after almost a decade together, and I moved to his home town before we had our son. Very shortly after he was born I realised that I needed to end our marriage and go it alone so that I could raise him in a happy home. It was the hardest, but most important decision I have ever made. From the outside, single parenting looked scary, impossible almost, and I felt shame and guilt that I wouldn't be raising my son in a two-parent household; not to mention the worries I had about making it work financially: I had to figure out a way to almost double my earnings if I was going to survive in the long term on my own.

For the first year after becoming a single parent, I basically hid away in my house, crocheting and not looking at my phone. Despite growing up in a happy household, headed by a wonderful single mother (shout out to Jackie, you calm and magical being), and having a diverse and beautiful family of step- and half-siblings, whom I adore, becoming a single mother felt like the worst possible outcome at the time. I didn't have friends or my own family close by, and I didn't know many other parents, let alone single parents, on whom I could lean or who could tell me that everything was going to be OK. I didn't have anyone to tell me that my little imperfect family was perfect, exactly as it was.

I wish I'd had something or someone to guide me, because I was navigating everything alone and making hundreds of mistakes along the way. Those mistakes taught me so much, but I wish I'd had a blueprint to steady me.

That is the goal of this book: to be that guide for all the newly single parents, the future single parents and the would-be single parents – to imperfectly guide you as you start life as the head of your own, perfect little family. Six years on, I have built a life I love. It has taken a lot of hard work, both in terms of my career (working twice as much and writing late into the night to make the finances work) and emotional work too. But I have incredible friends, and being single later in life has given me the freedom to start again from scratch and learn about myself, with a new motivation to find happiness: my beautiful son. I have dated, fallen in (and out of) love, come out as queer (in a newspaper – the normal way!) and had my heart and mind opened by being part of the incredibly diverse single-parenting community. The pieces I've written about single parenting and life as a single mum along the way are my second proudest achievements (behind my parenting itself) to date. When I became a single parent it felt like the breaking of me, but it's turned out to be the making. I have a sweet and happy little boy, and I am grateful for every moment that I get to be his happy single parent.

Stepping out of the box

Since becoming single mothers, we've met more incredible single parents than we ever imagined possible. The single mums and dads we've met along the way are, across the board, strong, kind, compassionate, tenacious and fierce. Through choice? Possibly, but more likely through necessity. Not wanting to sound all Dr Suess and 'Today is your day' about things, but the chances are that things are about to get a little bit wonderful. You will stumble, you may even fall, but you'll pick yourself up, brush yourself off and keep going, because you'll learn quickly that that's what single parents must do, and the learning curve is steep.

It's not all potholes and bruises, though – single parenthood is glorious too. It might not have been the way you envisaged your parenting journey. The chances are that it was a little bit more textbook in the planning stages, but we're going to let you in on a secret. 'Normal' is just a box. It's a box that society uses to keep things simple and to discourage anyone from rocking the boat. It is the box that we keep ourselves in so that we don't have to grow. Once you step outside the box – or someone else throws the box away, against your will, while you desperately cling to the edges – you will realise that you're now free to grow as big as you like. And your lucky child or children get to grow along with you. They'll grow up in a world without boxes too. They'll see how strong, how brave, how amazing their parent or parenting team is, and they'll benefit from realising that you don't have to follow the norm to thrive.

But let us not get ahead of ourselves; you've picked up this book (or been handed it by a kind and very clever friend) because you are at the start of your journey, thinking about making the leap, or hitting a rocky patch.

Becoming a parent is like being hit over the head with a hammer. Your old life has ended and your new one has begun. Becoming a *single* parent upgrades that hammer to a sledgehammer. You'll look around you and see happy, nuclear families with 2.4 children (that poor and peculiar 0.4 we never address) everywhere. They're in the park, they're on buses, outside schools, in restaurants, on beaches – you'll feel as if you have a neon sign over your head reading 'riding solo' or worse: 'failure'.

Well, from one 'failure' to another, let us tell you, there is nothing broken about your home. We are part of the 15 per cent (or more) of families headed by a single parent that makes up our weird and crowded species and spaces. We are divorcees, widows, widowers, separated parents, solo parents by choice, adoptive parents, queer solo parents, whatever label you have, we are simply people doing the job of two parents at once. Once you realise that you're not alone, you're simply home alone, you'll start realising that you've joined the most incredible and inspiring community that you may ever be a part of. In picking up this book, you've taken your first big step into that community.

From surviving the first few weeks to moving on, through legal matters, co-parenting negotiations or finding a helping hand as a solo parent and into dating and navigating work, these chapters will take you step by step through the first few days, weeks, months and years of your new life.

You are not alone

First things first, let's address the single elephant in the room. You see, as soon as we call the elephant 'single', you feel sorry for them. Single means 'only one, not one of several', an individual not a group, a solo, one of a kind, a singular entity. This sounds sad. It sounds lonely. It sounds isolating. This is because society has told us that being single is sad. Therefore, being a single parent is also sad. And no matter how many headlines you read that suggest this, we can categorically promise you that this is simply not true. The very title is arguably a misnomer. A single parent is not 'only one'. You will never be 'only one' again. You are one plus child or children. You are a family unit, a collection, a group – decidedly several.

We won't pretend that single parenting doesn't feel isolating at times. It might feel like you're now undertaking an enormous task on your own, it may be the very reason you picked up this book. But our most important message to you, even if it is the only one you take from this book (it won't be, we hope), is that you are *not* alone. The only thing that separates single parents from co-parenting teams is that we are solo heads of households. It feels isolating when you don't find your family set-up modelled in the people around you, your peers on the playground during drop-off and pick-up, or the families you see in the media. And while the challenges faced by different sectors under the single-parent-family umbrella are different, we want to remind you of what brings us all together. There are all kinds of families that fall under the single-parent umbrella, but we may refer to four main groups that together form our diverse and glorious community.

The four main groups of single-parent families

1 Divorced or separated single parents with a co-parent

The largest group of single parents are those facing life as the solo head of a family following the breakdown of a relationship with their child, or children's, other parent. Alongside adjusting to a new single life with kids, these parents have legal and financial hurdles to overcome in the untangling of a life previously shared. Many single parents in this group are also dealing with overcoming infidelity or domestic abuse. Healing from these experiences while navigating life as a newly single parent can be incredibly hard, and finding a dedicated support group of people in the same position can be hugely beneficial.

2 Single parent, not by choice

Some single parents don't choose to go it alone. Perhaps they find themselves pregnant unexpectedly and their partner chooses not to stick around. Perhaps the relationship broke down, or it didn't exist in the first place. Alongside the challenges of going it alone as the head of a new family, these single parents may be struggling to come to terms with a life unplanned.

3 Solo parent by choice

A solo parent by choice is a single parent who chooses to have a child or children on their own without the involvement of a co-parent. This is typically via sperm donor or adoption, depending on the situation and sex of the solo parent. Challenges faced by solo parents by choice include: the legal legwork involved in the road to becoming a parent; the sole financial responsibility for the family; and having no co-parent to share parenting, financial and childcare responsibilities with.

4 Widow/widower solo parents

Widows or widowers are solo parents who have become single parents after the death of the co-parent of their children. Additional challenges include navigating family grief alongside the legal and financial challenges of becoming the sole parent at the head of a family.

In all of these groups there are other factors at play that can add to the challenges. Single parents with disabilities face unique hurdles, or those parenting neurodivergent children or those with additional physical needs or disabilities. Those on low incomes (or no incomes) have an extra layer of things to think about. LGBQT+ solo and single parents have extra challenges when navigating social and legal issues, depending on where they are raising their children. Some expat single parents are now tied to another country away from their families, having split from a partner they moved abroad for.

We are all part of this varied and marvellous intersectional single-parent brigade. But what are the threads that hold this motley – and bright and inspiring – crew together? It is our shared goal: to be good parents to happy children. The love for our kids binds us. We all want the same things. We all *need* the same things: to find our way in a society built for two-person parenting teams, not just financially but socially, and to find a place for ourselves and our families – one that allows us to thrive. Through the unique and varying circumstances we all find ourselves in, we have shared experiences, worries and joys that bring us together.

In navigating these as a team, we can find community. Every single or solo parent has woken up on Mother's or Father's Day and been faced with an Instagram feed full of nuclear-family parents being spoilt by their kids (via the other parent) only to feel lost and lonely and faced with a day of the usual parenting duties for one. It is these moments that your single-parent community is here for. To remind you to put that bottle of champagne in the fridge the night before so that you can have a breakfast mimosa and celebrate yourself in the way you deserve. When you're feeling completely overwhelmed by the legal and financial climb to independence ahead of you, finding a group of solo-parent friends online going through the exact same thing means that you can share the mental load between you. You are not alone, despite your new solo title.

We (Zoë and Rebecca), in fact, met on Mother's Day at an event for Zoë's Frolo app launch, a room full of strangers united in single motherhood. We left that dinner with a phone full of lifelong friends, a network of support and a sign from the universe that each one of us was going to be OK. If you're reading this now, you're going to be OK, too, but how? How will you get to OK? How will you surpass OK and get to be the incredible, capable and strong parent you want to be?

We're going to guide you there throughout this book. Whatever your circumstances, you've ended up outside this uncomfortably tight box, and *this* is your chance to design a new one. With the help of this book, you'll be able to decide what you'd like family life to look like to you, and make it happen. We're going to start out by addressing all your challenges, fears and to-dos head on, with a series of practical tasks that will map out your plan to getting you where you want to be. By the time you've worked through this book, single parenting itself will be reframed to seem like a holiday: a quite active, adventure-style holiday, yes, but a holiday all the same.

Once we've worked through your immediate survival strategy by making The List in Chapter 1, we'll be systematically getting to grips with single parenthood and childcare, finances, work, legal considerations, stigma, friendships, holidays, dating and beyond. Yes, in the space of this short book, we promise we're going to convince you that single parenthood isn't something to 'survive' – it's a new and glorious chapter in your life that you deserve to enjoy and cherish.

Talking to the kids

However you're coming into single parenthood, the chances are your children might have questions about their situation. Unfortunately, non-traditional family set-ups are not frequently modelled (in a positive way at least) in the media or in books. For this reason, either at the start of your single-parenting journey or somewhere down the line, you'll need to speak to the children about their family set-up. If you're

entering your single-parenting journey as the result of a relationship breakdown, and your children are old enough to
ask questions, this conversation is likely to need to take place
sooner rather than later. The most important thing to remember in these discussions is that you don't have to have all the
answers. You just have to make the space for your children
to ask questions, and to have the opportunity to express their
emotions and feel seen and held with all their feelings.

If you're coming into single parenthood following a separation or divorce, Natalie Alexis Lee (@stylemesunday)
told us that asking your children how they're feeling centres
them in the conversation and helps them to understand that
it's not about them. She says: 'I think the best thing you can
do is ask open-ended questions; give them space to express
their feelings. It's really easy to get in our own heads about
what's going on for us at that time. And, in fact, they're just
the little people that are mixed up with all of this and they
have no choice. It's really important to keep checking in with
them to ask them how they're feeling about it. Check that they
are not internalising it and they don't think it's their fault.
These conversations aren't just one-off conversations that you
need to have. They need to be a continual thing. Kids are, by
design, egocentric, so if there's a change in circumstance, their
natural instinct is to blame themselves for it. It needs to be
vocalised repetitively that no, this is to do with us; we made
this decision. Then the best thing you can do is just to listen.'

This open communication is also relevant in other situations too. Widow Holly Matthews became a single mother
in her early thirties following the death of her husband Ross.
And she says nothing is off-limits when it comes to her children's questions: 'The one thing that I did was tell them that
they can ask me anything, and no questions are off limits.
No matter how many times I have to say it, no matter how

painful it is to me, they have to have space to have their feelings. And they have to have space to be angry, sad, want to break things, swear – anything.'

Whatever your circumstances, keeping the channel of communication open between you and your children is the most important thing. And don't be afraid to show them your emotions, as long as you aren't burdening them with the responsibility of holding them for you (if you're not able to do this yet, burden friends or family with them for now). Try to remember that the sooner you feel OK (or even good) about your single-parent status, the sooner your children are likely to feel OK about their family set-up too. That's all the more reason to focus on getting happy yourself.

Get happy

When you picked up this book, you may have felt that there was very little tethering you to the possibility of being OK again. You might have frantically googled 'famous widowers' or 'successful single parents' or 'how many nannies does Angelina Jolie have as a single mother of six' and come away feeling even more despondent than when you started. Yes, it's helpful in theory to see other single parents out in the world and doing well and being happy, but, right now, at this point in your journey when you can't see how to get there, an element of 'compare and despair' theory creeps in.

How did they get there? How, oh how, can they possibly be coping, nay, happy as a solo parent, or a co-parent who spends nights or even weeks away from their kids? Allow them to inspire you, if you can, because that is all ahead of you too. But if you can't, look away. For the moment, it's time to turn off social media and allow us to guide you through the first steps in your journey to solo-parenting success. For some, seeing single parents living their best lives will offer them hope, but if it makes you feel resentful, overwhelmed, exasperated or simply confused, stop looking outwards and look inwards for a little while. If you've just had an emergency C-section, the last thing you need is to read a blog post about an at-home water birth from a green-juice-sipping influencer. If you're mid-divorce, you don't want to browse bridal magazines. Take a step back and focus on yourself. For every single parent loving life – and telling you how much they love it – there is another frantically trying to stay afloat, and we're here to help you move from this group into the loving-life category. We're here to help you get happy.

Remember this and this alone on days when you just don't know how to do this: happy parents make happy kids.

You deserve to be happy in your own right. Do you want your children to grow up in a world where the only option for success and happiness is to fit the picture of family life painted by someone else? Or do you want them to have the option to make their own choices? Whether you have chosen it, or single parenthood has been forced upon you, you are now breaking the mould. You have the opportunity to colour outside the lines, to throw away the picture completely and paint your own beautiful. You are Jackson Pollock. You are Georgia O'Keefe. Not only does this open up a world of limitless opportunity for the rest of your life but it also gives you the chance to model something exciting and beautiful for your children.

They won't have to do things by the book, either. They don't have to fit into society's versions of success. They won't have to wait for Prince or Princess Charming to pick them to fulfil their dreams of parenthood. They won't feel obliged to start a family just because that's 'the done thing'. The 'done thing' will be the pursuit of happiness, whatever the situation. They won't stay in an unhappy home because there's no viable alternative. They'll know there is. By finding happiness as a single parent, you're showing them that they can defy the odds, go against the grain, overcome adversity and be stronger than they ever thought possible. Finding happiness in single parenthood is not only vital for you but also inspirational for your children.

Throughout this book, we'll tell you how we've muddled through, but, more importantly, we'll introduce you to our team of experts, and our diverse and brilliant group of single and solo parents from all walks of life, who will share their single-parent stories with us, to help you get it right first time. Yes, the traditional way of raising a baby in our society might be with two parents, but, dammit, it *does* take a village and you're about to learn that there's no village more welcoming (or, admittedly, messier) than this happy single-parent mega-commune you've just moved into.

Welcome.

My single-parent story

Helen Thorn, divorced co-parent and part of the comedy duo Scummy Mummies. Helen is also author of Get Divorced, Be Happy

My story was a big surprise. I became a single parent in March 2020, just before the pandemic. I found out that my ex-husband had been having an affair for four years with a woman I knew of, but hadn't met, and my world kind of shattered. We'd been together for 22 years; we met when I was 19 and were married for ten years. We were five days off signing a big mortgage to renovate our house. I just thought that was it, that I would be married for ever and ever and ever. I went into absolute shutdown and shock, and then he left the next day after I found out: I kicked him out. I instantly became a single parent, and then the pandemic happened a couple of weeks later. So, I was sort of thrust into a situation where I was dealing with grief and heartbreak and betrayal, but also there was the home-schooling isolation and I didn't have a hug from an adult for three months. It felt like a kind of bootcamp of single parenting because I was with my kids five days a week; he had them at the weekends. But we quickly adapted into this new family of three. The kids were eight and 11 at the time, so they were old enough that I could tell them what had happened. I sort of appreciated that I went into single parenting in that chaotic way, because it was sink or swim. I loved having that intense time.

I think the stigma is what holds people back from getting divorced. They think: *It's lonely, I can't afford it. I'll get a smaller house.* And they'll just list all the negatives. And that's what I wanted to do with the book and Instagram, and the radio and podcasting work that I do, to say 'I've never felt so happy.' And I've always said that it's the happiness that I thought I would get, and the security and the comfort and the love that I thought I would get from a marriage. It's actually what I get from being alone.

Freedom is the greatest prize of being a single parent.

Helen's advice

I get so many people who want reassurance. They'll say, 'I've just found out my husband's been having an affair with my best friend. How do I get through this?' My first response is: reach out for help. People will love you. People will support you. It's going to be very hard, but it will be the best thing that's ever happened to you. And you are free. You are now free. And don't worry about what they're up to with their new partner. Because they'll never be happy. And you will be, and you are loved.

1

Tick, Tick, Tick, Tick, Boom! – Making The List

'The only way around is through.'

Robert Frost

This chapter is the first step in changing everything. One of the most common problems facing the single-parent community is being overwhelmed, so we have to tackle that feeling before we can tackle anything else. If you're feeling overwhelmed, or you know that you have a thousand things to do but just the thought of doing any one of them is too much, we're going to face that feeling head on. If you know, logically, that there is a future in which things make sense but picturing it in any detail is impossible, that changes here.

The list you'll make in this section of the book feels hard and huge, but it will become your parenting bible. The List is your toolkit for days when everything feels like too much and you want to bury your head in the sand; it's your guide to handling the bad days better and knowing what a good day looks like for you.

This chapter is a practical one. We're going to present you with things to consider and questions to answer. Take your time with these and don't do them all in one go. Work through them over the course of a few days and give them the space, time and thought that they deserve. This is about getting all your worries, thoughts, plans, hopes, dreams and ideas down on paper so that they are out of your head, and you can find the space for some mental peace and clarity. If you're some way into your single-parenting journey and settled into a routine, you may be able to skip parts of this process, but there's always room for improvement, so continue with an open mind.

The List is your own personal route to happiness. Your fairway to freedom. Your course to contentment. Your pathway to peace. The List is the biggest, most intimidating, but most empowering to-do list of every single parent's life, and though it will look slightly different to everyone, making it is the first step at surviving – nay, thriving – as a single parent. The starting point is where you might have been when you picked up this book. We'll call it point A. Point A often involves flailing; it is a place of confusion and feeling overwhelmed, of self-doubt and, at times, despair. But The List leads us to point B. Point B is better. It is no longer flailing. It is a place of keeping calm and collected, and of carrying on. It is the jumping-off point to the rest of your life as the head of your perfectly imperfect family.

NOTE Before we embark on the list-making portion of the aforementioned-oft-mentioned-after List, if you don't feel ready to answer questions just yet, feel free to continue with a few more chapters of the book and get familiar with some of your options in the areas of childcare, legal obligations and finances before circling back to this more practical section of the book. Realistically, this is the most important part of getting set up as a happy single parent, but we realise that you might be feeling a little ill-equipped just now. Forge ahead, or read Chapters 2–6, before circling back to the next bit and making your pathway to freedom. We encourage a 'choose your own adventure' approach to reading this book – and to parenting.

Part I – before we make The List

Making The List is all about answering the first and most important question for all single parents, whatever your situation: 'How will I cope? How will I make myself strong enough to be the single parent my child deserves?' Because the truth is, what you're embarking on *is* scary. You are now, whether full- or part-time, solely responsible for the safety, wellbeing and happiness of at least one other human. It all rests on you, so how *will* you cope? By the time this chapter ends, you will have a plan.

First, let's focus on the now: putting one foot in front of the other. You need to build your self-care toolkit to get you through the next hours, days, weeks, months. We're soon going to be asking you a series of questions to help you work out the basis of your list, so to give you the idea, we thought that you might have some for us first. The following questions are the ones that filled our heads when we became single parents, so if these are what are keeping you awake right now, let's try to work through some tough questions together so that we can move on to the practical issues at hand.

How do I get through this?

Answer: with this book. We are here to guide you. It's a very steep and very sudden learning curve, but the trick is to know that you're not alone. Up to a quarter of all parents have been through this; thousands are doing it right now, this second, at the same time as you. In this, the hardest time, you need to focus simply on staying afloat. Feed yourself and your child, clean yourself and your child, put your child to bed and go to bed yourself. Eat, sleep, repeat. Make cups of tea, let them go cold as you stare out the window, reheat them in the microwave and then do it again. Stroke your child's back as they watch *Peppa Pig*. Simply get through the immediate future by doing what you need to do and focusing on the very next task at hand.

How do I keep going when it's all too much?

Answer: allow your child to guide you. A quest for your own happiness is noble and brilliant and courageous, but if you can't muster it right now, be motivated by the quest for theirs.

How will I explain my child's situation to them?

Answer: the truth is you probably don't need to do that right now. It's something every single or solo parent thinks about from the off, but right now, your child just needs to know that they are safe, and that you are OK. If you have older kids and you've just separated from their other parent, you may need to explain that they'll be spending some time apart from one or other of you in the near future, but when it comes to divorce, co-parenting, adoption, surrogates, whatever your unique and beautiful circumstances, your child doesn't need a full and complete explanation right now, not until you're able to give one. Ask them questions, rather than presuming to answer ones they may not have.

What have I got to look forward to?

It can feel bleak; we've been there: Christmas Days alone, sitting in an empty living room after bedtime, the prospect of budget beach breaks with nobody to apply sun cream to your back. You're allowed a tiny bit of self-pity and doom-dreaming, but we're only allowing a little.

In fact, you can answer this one yourself; let's do two quick tasks to get you started.

Task 1 Write down all the terrible future things you're worrying about or predicting. These worries and fears are probably swirling around in your mind and stopping you from having the mental space to address more pressing issues. Let's get them out of your head and down onto paper. You can then throw it in the bin if you like or tuck it away at the back of this book, or in a cupboard ready to laugh about in a year or so when you're content and smug.

Task 2 Now that Task 1 is out of your system, get at least three things in your diary that you can look forward to:
One short term This should be something very small but that you know will give you great pleasure, with minimum effort and very few hurdles. How about a coffee with a friend, a long bubble bath, a solo run, or a pint with a mate?
One medium term This might be something that requires a little more organising, but it should be a worthy reward for the progress you will have made by this point. Perhaps a hotel stay with or without your child, a live sports event, a theatre trip, or a night out in an actual bar?
And one long term (the one for when you've ticked off the majority of The List) Dream big for this one. When you're settled into your new life as a happy single parent, you're going to want to celebrate. How about a family holiday, buying

yourself that watch or bag you've always wanted, or a dinner party with all your friends and family?

Having treats in mind to keep you focused is a must. Self-care is not a luxury: it is a necessity. We cannot pour from an empty cup, and if you are thinking only about, and acting for, your child at all times, you're going to burn out.

One last question for us that might be on your mind: 'Am I ever going to be OK again?'

Yes. We promise. Better than OK, you're going to be wonderful.

Question time

Now it's time for you to answer some important questions that, collectively, will form the basis of your List. You thought you were a pro at making lists (to-do lists, shopping lists, Christmas lists – er bucket lists?), but now you're a single parent, you're going to need to up your game. Your daily to-do list is about to be twice as long with half the necessary people to manage it, and you'll likely never quite work your way through it all ('clean out fridge' and 'wash PE kit' dangle perilously off the end of many a single parent's Sunday task sheet). But before you get bogged down in the minutiae of listing and relisting, let us start with the most important list of all.

Ready? Part II – making The List

Are you now sold on The List? Let's begin. Unlike other lists, you won't be able to make this in chronological or task order. It may be necessary to start at the end and work backwards. This is an exercise in unravelling. To find out exactly what you need, right now, to nail this new and vitally important job, we need to ask some really big questions. Everyone's circumstances are different, as is what makes happy single parenting possible for you, but across the board the key considerations are: home, financial security, childcare and learning to love your life. This part of the book is challenging but rewarding. Treat yourself to a beautiful new notebook in which to hold all your hard work. Collect the drawings from your child's nursery and make a scrap paper book. Download a fancy list app (such as 'To Do') if you prefer to go digital. Hell, write them on the back of your wedding photos you've just taken out of frames (too soon?). Just keep it all together in one place, take your time and think long and hard about your answers, and reward yourself after every section you complete.

Home

You'll need somewhere to live. Thinking about what your family home set-up looks like for these first few weeks, months, years of single parenting is essential, and this forms one strand of considerations for The List. This will change over time, your kids will grow, there will be schools, nurseries, and jobs to think about, but don't get bogged down in that. This is about the physical living space you and your child or children need right now, to be comfortable and safe.

If you're separating from a partner, your ex will also need somewhere to live, so there may be short-term or interim elements to the home part of your list. Don't forget that you may need help with living costs, even if just in the short term, and wherever you are living there will be support systems in place to ensure you and your child have somewhere safe to call home.

You're about to learn the true meaning of that old adage 'home is where the heart is'. No, it might not be the Ritz, it might not be Barbie's Dream Home (just us?), but when you lock that front door and put your child to bed and sit down with a cup of tea in your very own space, it will feel like you're exactly where you belong.

Have a go at these questions now. Take your time with them, and any that you're not able to answer – or ready to think about – come back to later.

Questions to answer now (not all will be relevant to everyone)

What is the most basic home that you need for yourself and your child/ren to be safe? How many rooms do you need and what does it need to have in it? Where could it be?

- Where are you currently living?
- Is it safe?
- Can you stay there?
- How long for?
- Do you want to?
- What are your living options?

If you're renting:

- Can you pay the rent alone?
- How will you pay next month's rent?
- Do you feel confident that you'll be able to continue paying this in the long term?

If you own your house or have a mortgage:

- Can you pay the mortgage and bills alone?
- Can you continue covering these mortgage costs on your own in the long term?
- Do you need a new mortgage?
- Is there an ex in the picture?
- If yes, where will they go if they move out, or where will you go if it's you that's leaving?
- Do you live close to any support? Think about friends, family and childcare settings.
- What other support networks do you need?
- Do you picture yourself living where you are now in the long term?
- What three things would your ideal home set-up include? Think about space, location and facilities.

Financial and legal security

Let's talk money. Remember, this chapter isn't about solving your problems; it's about identifying everything you need to think about so that you can make a plan to do so. Money is a topic that many people try to avoid thinking and talking about as much as possible, but for single parents finding their way, it's really common to go from feeling muddled to over-whelmed in the blink of an eye. Getting money-savvy is no longer optional.

This strand of The List might be about taking on extra work or a new job, asking for flexible working, sorting out child-maintenance payments, working out the welfare system or just getting really, *really* good at picking lottery numbers. (The last strategy is not recommended, but if it works for you, can you lend us a fiver?)

We will be dealing with finances in a later chapter, so for now it's about the immediate future. In the short term, you will need to make changes to your spending, because although former single mum Jennifer Lopez was right when she said 'Love Don't Cost a Thing', kids do. It's time to answer some more questions now, so put the kettle on and get your notebook out again. Remember to take your time with this and come back to any you're not sure about right now. There's no need to make a full budget immediately (that's a point for The List), but your answers to these questions will help you with what to put on it.

Questions to answer now (skip any that don't apply)

Outgoings What are your current outgoings? Remember to include things like rent, bills, food, childcare, phone, and so on.

- What are your monthly/annual earnings?
- Can you cover bills on your own? (If the answer is no, don't panic, we'll be covering options to address this later.)
- What will new or additional childcare costs be?

Legal/financial considerations

- If you've lost your partner, do you have a financial advisor to work through accounts, investments and insurance policies?
- Do you have any inheritance or insurance money that you will need to invest and manage to ensure the security of your family? Do you have a plan for this or will you need to make one?
- Do you have a will?

- If you need them, are your adoption papers completed?
- Do you have house, car, life, medical insurance?

Co-parents

- Have you got an ex- or co-parent who will contribute to child maintenance?
- Do you think they will they do so voluntarily?

Savings

- Do you have savings? How much?
- Do you have any other financial-security nets, such as income protection insurance or stocks or investments?
- Make a list of as many financial assets you can think of that you currently have.
- Can family help? Could someone lend you money or provide accommodation or free childcare support for you?
- Can you explore loan options?

Income

- Do you need to increase your salary or take on additional work?
- Do you need to cut your hours or request flexible working?
- Do you currently receive any extra state financial support?
- Will you qualify for financial aid, housing support or other state help?

Don't worry if answering these questions has thrown up a lot more questions. Finding out the answers to these will form the basis of The List. Remember, this is about getting everything down on paper so that you can find order and mental clarity. We know how hard answering these questions can feel, but these issues are weighing on your mind whether you're addressing them or not. Writing them down on paper so that they are out of your head and you can find order in the answers will significantly reduce the stress. If it feels as if you're being pulled into the quicksand of chaos, keep answering these questions and making the lists, and single parenting will be a walk on the beach in no time.

Childcare

Whether it's negotiating for your ideal co-parenting set-up or finding a local babysitter to give you a couple of hours a week for a peaceful bath, childcare is, or will be, essential to your life as a single parent. This might be in formal settings such as schools or nurseries, or family members who will form part of your extended parenting team, but thinking about what your childcare set-up will look like feeds into your decision about where and how you'll set up home, so you need to be mindful of this from the beginning.

If you're navigating a split, the status quo you maintain off the bat may end up becoming permanent if you fall into a rhythm with it, so think carefully about not only what works best for you, but first and foremost what will be best for the kids. This is why we need to be ordered and methodical in how we are making these decisions. If you're entering single parenting further into your parenting career with older kids, you'll likely need to rely on your outside childcare providers in new ways, whether it's roping in your parents for a weekly sleepover at Granny or Grandad's, or signing up for extra after-school club sessions so that you can get through all your meetings. Thinking about who might be able to offer assistance in the short and long term is a key element of The List. And if you're entering single parenthood as a solo parent, remember that aside from time to work, you will need time off too. Even if it's just for an hour (or a week, that's fine too), at some point you'll require some time alone to recharge.

We've got some more questions for you now. Remember to take a break so that you're not trying to tackle all these topics at once, and skip over any that don't apply to you.

Questions to answer now

General

- Name three things you'll need childcare for. Think about things like work, dating, extra meetings, weddings, the gym.
- Can you name three people who could help you in an emergency?
- How about a non-emergency?

Co-parenting (skip this if you're not navigating another parent)

- Do you have an ex who will be co-parenting with you?
- Do you have a set-up in practice since the split?
- What is your gut feeling about how you will split time? Fifty/fifty? Every other weekend? Once a month?
- What would your ideal set-up look like?
- What do you think the kids would want?
- What do you think would work well for them in the short term?

- And the long term?
- If they're older, have you asked them what they think?
- Will your co-parent cooperate, do you think?
- Will there be flexibility for you both to swap days when needed? (Be honest about whether this would work for both of you.)
- Are you married?
- Do you plan on getting divorced?
- Will you need a court order or mediation?

Childcare settings

- Do you have existing childcare support?
- What is, or do you think will be, their main childcare setting? Nursery? School? Family? Nanny?
- Do you have family nearby who would help when you need a break?
- Does your child currently have a childcare setting or are they in full-time education?
- Do you live near your child's childcare setting?
- How will you get them there and back?
- Where will the kids be while you work?
- How will school holidays and dates such as religious or bank holidays work?

Non-essential childcare

- How will you ensure that you get some time to yourself outside working hours?
- What three things would you do for yourself if childcare wasn't an issue? Think about holidays, bubble baths, runs, walks, book clubs, football matches – anything your heart desires.

- What childcare would you need to make
  them happen?

Guardianship

- Now, let's think about guardianship. Who would
  you want to take care of your children in the event
  something happens to you?
- Have you got a document set out specifying
  your wishes?

As we mentioned earlier, it's important to keep in mind that
your childcare needs change relatively quickly as your child
grows and as your work or home situation evolves. Right now,
it's about the childcare you need for the first year or so of single
parenthood, and getting any co-parenting set-ups in place. You
can revisit this annually, or as and when you need to change
things, but it's a lot easier to identify how to do this when you
have a steady base that you and the kids are happy with, which
you've actively decided upon.

Life

On to easier, more lovely things. On to building a life you
love. And while the stresses of home, money and childcare
responsibilities might feel overwhelming, don't forget why
you're doing all this, why you're reading a book about how to
be a happy single parent in the first place. It's for the love of a
child, for your children. As you make The List, remember that
you're doing this to help you start your new life as a family, a
life that is filled with love.

Point B on the list shouldn't look like 'coping', it should
look like a healthy, happy, love-filled life that you want to

be living. Before we make The List, we have one more set of questions for you to ask yourself, and these ones aren't about survival, they're about building your new life. Once you've defined what this looks like for you, you can start to work backwards and unpick each and every tangle between your situation now and that glorious state of togetherness.

We know, we've asked you to answer a lot of questions already, but these ones really are important. There is just one last topic to address before we encourage you to look at all your answers. The final (and we think most important) set of needs to consider when making The List not only provide you with the things to think about to create your support system but also your self-care toolkit and plan of action for the tough times, because some of this stuff is heavy. Some of you may be entering a whole new world of things to think about after making the beautiful decision to become a solo parent by choice and feel amped up for the challenge.

Others will be applying for divorce after adultery, negotiating a co-parenting set-up with an abuser or working through finances after the death of a partner. We are here to guide each and every one of you through these things. You are not alone, as lonely as you might feel. There will be days when The List we're about to make will feel too long and too difficult to face, where the task of getting up and putting one foot in front of the other at all will feel like too much. Those are the days we're here for. Those are the days we need to plan for now, before we're in them, because the kids are reliant on you and you alone now. We started off thinking about your immediate self-care toolkit for the early days, and now we need long-term coping plans. We need a plan for *life*. This is the section for when you hit a hurdle, and we'll ask you to answer these questions so that you can keep the answers ready for when you stumble, to ensure that it doesn't turn into a fall.

Your self-care plan – questions to answer now

- What is the absolute minimum you can do to get by in a day? (When you hit a hard day, do the things on this list and nothing else.)
- What do the kids need, like *really* need from you? Meals, someone to wash and dress them, a hug?
- If you can't give it to them, what will you do?
- How could you prepare for the hard days? Could you freeze meals for when you're tired? Prep a neighbour to be an emergency contact? Ask a parent to come and stay?
- Name three things that will keep the kids happy if you need a break. (Yes, they can all be screens, but perhaps there are other options?)
- What is the minimum *you* need to be happy on an average day?
- What would success as a single parent look like to you? (Perhaps it's a Friday night cosied up on the sofa watching a movie with the kids. Maybe it's paying each and every bill without any help each month. Maybe it's being the next Erin Brockovich. Aim high.)
- Write down three feelings you'll have when you're settled into your single-parent life. Relieved? Excited? Contented?
- Write down three ways you might talk to your kids about their situation.
- Do you have a single-parent support network? (You'll need one – more on this later.)
- What's your favourite treat? (Have one now, go on.)

Self-care

- Name three things you can do to feel a little better when you're low. Think about things like journaling, meditation, exercise or resting.
- What's your favourite place?
- How could you make your home feel like a sanctuary?
- Write down three things you like about yourself.
- What are three things you're good at?
- Name three people you will call when you need help. (If you wrote nobody, we need to address this right away. Give it some thought and be sure there really is *nobody* you can lean on for help. If you truly don't have anyone who can help, one of the first points on your list will be to address this.)

Well done, you're now a little better prepared for the rough patches. We'll be honest, the rough patches might be less 'patchy' and more 'entire periods of life'. You might need to hibernate for a little while, stop talking to anyone but the kids plus your best mate or your mum (we've covered this, you're not allowed to cut yourself off completely) and learn a useless new hobby such as crochet or calligraphy (tick and tick) for a while until you feel ready to rejoin the real world. We grow up being told that a successful family looks like a mum and dad, plus children, so the fact that your beautiful little family doesn't fit the mould might leave you feeling guilty, ashamed, confused or grieving. We'll help you with this later in the book. Don't beat yourself up for feeling any or all these things, acknowledge that that's understandable and then also acknowledge that what you're about to do is rebuild your family in a way that actually works. You're about to prove that rules were made to be broken. (Everyone loves a rebel.)

Find your people

Speaking of rebels, misfits, rule-breakers and miscreants, it's time to find your people. The only thing making you feel that your family doesn't fit the mould is looking at too many families from a different batch. One in four families is a single-parent family. Yes, roughly 25 per cent, so where are they? If you were one of the people who answered that you didn't have anyone who could help you, this part is twice as important.

Number two on your list (number one being making The List itself) should be finding your people. Mum and dad friends are all well and good but when they're bitching about their partners and telling you you're 'so lucky' you don't have to deal with relationship dramas, you *will* want to kill them. Find your single-parent crew immediately. If you don't know where to start, sign up to the Frolo app, find a local parenting Facebook group, do some investigating in the playground. As soon as you're part of an inclusive community of single parents, you'll know you've found your people, and navigating the behemoth of a list alone will no longer seem so, well, lonely.

You'll also have a pool of resources for the stickier items on your list, from finding legal support to registering for universal credit or navigating telling your friends and family that you're becoming a solo parent by choice. We can't state enough how enormous the relief of finding your allies is, and once you're a member of the single-parenting group you'll realise that this community is more supportive, loving and loyal than any partner you've ever met. They have your back on the days that ticking off the next item of The List feels impossible.

Here's how you make The List

We feel fairly certain that you understand the importance of The List now, so let's make it. You've got 'Make list' and 'Find single parent crew' on there, and your mystical point B is dangling somewhere carrot-like a few lines or pages away, ready to be achieved just as soon as possible. It might feel like an impossible destination but, believe us, you will get there.

Here's how to take the answers to your questions and turn them into The List. Work through your answers and absolutely anything that requires attention should be adapted into a task for The List.

Example If you answered no to 'Do you have a will?', add 'Make will' to your list. If you answered yes to 'Do you need a new mortgage?', add 'Find a mortgage advisor' to The List.

Add absolutely everything you can think of related to each element of your goal. Answering the questions we've laid out for you above will have thrown up a lot of sticking points. These sticking points form the basis of your list. They are the things you need to know, research or action, and these should make up the tasks on your list. Use the answers to come up with your to-dos that will allow you to solve the problem in hand. Once you have all the tasks written down, you can prioritise them and make an ordered, detailed list that will map out your journey to success. This will form your completed version of The List.

Another example At this point you should be adding all your childcare tasks to The List. Do you need to sort childcare so that you can return to work as a solo parent? Consider tasks such as 'Set out working hours and compare nanny vs childminder vs nursery settings' and 'Submit application for childcare costs contributions'. Remember that if you're confused by any of these sections, you can read ahead to the relevant chapters to consider your options and then circle back to making The List.

Next on The List should be financial considerations. Consult the answers to our questions above and think about everything you need to address to be able to cope on your own financially. Your individual financial situation will be unique, but whatever they are, making a budget will be on every single-person's list. A good old-fashioned Excel spreadsheet should do the trick, add your incomings and every single one of your outgoings, from rent or mortgage payments to bills, subscriptions, childcare costs (that you've just been working out thanks to The List), food, car, clothes, your Sunday paper, your tube fares – the works.

We'll cover making your budget more fully in Chapter 4, but for many single parents, going through your finances will surface yet more tasks for The List. You will need to be creative in how you can make savings, but be realistic about what simply can't budge. Your living situation is non-negotiable, and how and where you live is inextricably tied to your financial situation, so nailing down exactly what is needed to secure a safe place for you and the kids to live is the key objective here.

Example If you answered yes to 'Do you need to increase your salary or take on additional work?', the tasks for your list will include things such as: 'Set up pay review meeting', 'Ask work about extra shifts', 'Speak to recruiters' or 'Speak to fellow single parents about how they increased their earnings.' Some single parents find that having no other adults in the house in the evening suddenly opens up time after bedtime for ad hoc overtime or additional jobs that can be done from home.

Next, you should review the answers to your questions about legal matters and create tasks from these for The List. Right now, you need to make sure that yourself and your child are legally protected. Have you got life insurance? A will? A guardianship plan in place? Your legal support needs will be different depending on your set-up, but the chances are you would benefit from some advice. 'Find a family lawyer' might find it's way on to your list, but we'd recommend reading our legal chapter (Chapter 6) before getting stuck into legal matters. Untangling a two-person parenting team to go solo is a little trickier on the legal front, so if this is you, your list will need a fair few actions to get you from point A to point B. Get. Them. On. The. List. (And read our legal chapter before you action them.)

By now that list is looking pretty comprehensive. You should be starting to see just how you're going to do this on your own. No, it's not going to be easy, but piece by piece, step by step, tick by tick on The List, you'll get there. Of course, we know that you'll have other lists. The daily to-do lists of single parents up and down the land spilleth over.

But how do I get this done?

You've made The List, but how do you actually work through it, when you're also busy single parenting? Try to take one or two items from The List and add them to the mix of your daily to-do list. Allot time to each task so that you make sure you get round to them. Pepper in easier tasks (sending an email) on your busier days with bigger ones (comparing childcare options) on your quieter ones, and don't always add them at the end of your daily task lists. Make them the first thing you do each day, as even if the race feels long, it is only by taking these small steps that you'll reach that finish line. Eliminate that 30-minute doom-scroll in the morning and check in your progress on The List. Reward yourself whenever you tick something off. If the promise of a toy at the end of a week of no bed-hopping can sleep-train a five-year-old, a chocolate biscuit for sending an email seems like the adult equivalent.

It is very important to mix in tasks from The List with your everyday jobs, so manage these jobs in the same way that you stay organised in day-to-day life. If you are a digital-first fan, integrate the list into your chosen task-managing app: To Do, Things and TickTick are all options to keep you accountable. If you're a 'scribble things down on Post-its' kinda person, add your tasks into your morning scribbles. Just make sure they're at the top.

There will be stumbling blocks in The List, and some tasks just won't seem to budge. Whether it's waiting for someone to sign something and they're dragging their heels, or it's an issue with a house move, or a backed-up court that just doesn't seem to be moving on your application, these tests will come and go, but with each day that passes, thanks to your list, you can be sure that you're still on track for success.

Freedom beckons

So to your new and wonderful life, and learning to love it. That fourth element of The List that we asked you to keep in mind as you made it. How about adding it to The List itself? How about adding tasks that remind you to treat yourself with love? A phone call to a friend. A long bubble bath once the kids are in bed. Your first post-single-parenthood night out with your best mate. Your first walk along the river with your baby as a solo parent. The first reading (nay, performance) of your favourite childhood book to the child you've fought so hard to be able to give your love to.

You've listed the things that make you happy, now set yourself reminders to do them as you work through The List. These milestones should be celebrated and commemorated – these milestones belong on your list of achievements. Once you've made and completed The List, there will be others. These will be much more fun to make, and even more fun to work through. They will help you navigate your first holiday as a single parent, get you through setting up your first online dating profile and being wined and dined, romanced, even ghosted and doing it all again. They will see you reluctantly planning the first night you take off from single parenthood, to counting down your hours until freedom and working your way through an epic list of unimaginable activities that only a single parent enjoying time off from their everyday life could find the energy for.

Your life will be full of lists, full of goals and dreams, failures and triumphs, but this first list, The List, is the one that will set you free.

The other list – our favourite things about being a single parent

OK, making The List felt a little heavy, didn't it? So, before we move on to some of the other heavy lifting of this book, we thought we'd pause and list a few of our favourite things about being a single parent that you might have ahead of you too.

Rebecca's list

- The school run is my favourite time of day. I walk home with Jack, his hand in mine, and tell him about my day, which prompts him to tell me about his. When we put the key in the lock of our front door, our little home is just ours.
- My son has a beautiful relationship with his grandma, my own single mum, and his granny, another single mum. Those two women have always shown up for me, and they show up for Jack week in, week out, reminding me that it doesn't take two adults to fill a house with love, and that it takes more than two parents to raise a child, whoever lives at home with them.
- I love my nights off, and weekends away with friends. I hated being away from my son for even a second in the early days, but now I feel very lucky to have a slice of freedom to recharge, explore, travel and play while Jack spends time in his second home with his dad or with his extended family.

- I love the feeling of strength and accomplishment that the role of single mother has brought into my life. Nothing else has made me feel so capable of achieving my dreams, or helping my son to achieve his. Financially, physically and emotionally, it is hard work, but you cannot put a price on the freedom, or the pride.
- Nothing, and I mean nothing, deserves a place on my list of favourite things about single motherhood more than my 'morning snug' with my son (or I get it in the evening on the couple of mornings a week that he doesn't wake up at home with me). Whatever stresses I have going on, for that little (or long) snug of time, nothing else exists in the world.
- And, of course, I love my single-parent friends, which brings us on to . . .

Zoë's list

- I love our adventures together. One of my favourite things has turned out to be one of the things I dreaded as a single parent: holidays for just the two of us. I love making space once a year for some time far away from everyone and everything – just Billy and me. I feel so lucky to be able to share these adventures and make these special memories with him, and it makes me feel that we are a little team.
- This brings me on to our bond. As a single parent, I feel that the bond we have is really strong and unique. Our home is a sanctuary and a place where we both feel happy and safe.

- I have come to love and appreciate the richness we get from this single-parent experience, from our frolo friends and the lovely experiences we share together from birthdays to Christmases to holidays. And because of our other friends and the extended family and community we have built via Frolo, I feel proud of dismantling the outdated social rule for my son (that would naturally make him feel 'other') that being a nuclear family is the 'right' way. I feel proud of the woman and mum I am and the challenges I have overcome because of it, and that Billy gets to witness it as he grows up.
- I have loved realising that I am stronger and more capable than I ever imagined, and that I have my own back no matter what. We might not be a nuclear family, but Billy and I are still our own little family unit, and it is our version of perfect.

2

They Who Must Not Be Named – The Other Parent

'The first thing I always say to people is: "You're a parent first, you're not a co-parent." When we hear the term "co-parent", we automatically start to think about the other parent and the dynamic with that person. But our role is to parent, to raise this child from infancy to adulthood. Co-parent just means that me and the other parent are no longer together. That's the only difference; my role hasn't changed. All that energy you have, all that frustration you have, take that energy and put it into your child, just spend more time with your child, you'll feel so much better because you're engaging with your child; your child's engaging with you. And you'll realise this is what it's about. That's the key: being child focused, just remain focused on the child, whatever is going on.'

Aaron Dale, founder of raisingboys_2men

When you raise your child alongside their other parent, it is most frequently referred to as 'co-parenting', and at other points in this book that is how you'll most commonly find references to a two-parent situation; however, we recognise that it doesn't always feel as if you're a team.

Co-parenting is a term that simply doesn't apply to some set-ups. Your child or children's other parent, or parents, may be involved in their lives but they may be on completely different scripts when it comes to how to parent, or what your child needs. In these instances, co-parenting might be impossible, in which case a technique called 'parallel parenting' comes into play.

The other parent might be technically referred to as your co-parent here, but once you know that they are in fact a *parallel* parent, and you are able to let go of the tie (and any expectation between you), existing in this way becomes a lot easier for you, and a lot less stressful for your children. Aside from how different or alike your parenting styles are, co-parenting can throw up a host of different bridges to cross and barriers to overcome, and in this chapter we'll be running through a handful of them for you to think about. First, let's recap those co-parenting styles.

Parallel parenting

Let's cover this option first, since if you're coming into single parenting with an ex, the chances are there may be some friction between you and your children's other parent at the beginning of your journey. In an ideal world you could approach parenting as a team and keep things completely consistent for the kids at both their homes, with shared routines, great communication on all fronts and zero conflict. But for one reason or another this is sometimes just not possible.

When you are not able to approach parenting as a team with your children's other parent, parallel parenting is a method that you can turn to. It might just be something you employ short term while you are both finding your feet as single parents, something you come back to when you hit a conflict or a rocky patch, or it might be the forever parenting method that works for your family.

Parallel parenting essentially means viewing yourself as running parallel, rather than in tandem, with your child's other parent. It means letting go of how your children are parented in their other home, accepting that it might be different from how things run in your home, and just making sure that they have a safe, consistent and loving home when they are with you. We'll stress that point again (now, and later), because if you can get the hang of it, it is truly revolutionary.

It is about *letting go* of what is happening at your children's other parent's home. You cannot control your ex, or how they parent. You cannot control how your children are parented when they are with your co-parent. As soon as you let go, *really* let go, of trying to maintain that control, you'll feel instantly more at peace.

So much parenting advice (which is, *quelle surprise*, situated on traditional family set-ups) is based on how children thrive on routine. We are told again and again that children find comfort and safety in routines, so when you have an ex who won't reply to your messages, who insists on letting the kids stay up late, who fails to brush their teeth, or who never does any reading with them, it can feel as if you have a duty to your children to enforce order in their other home. It is just one more area in which we can find an extra burden of single-parent guilt, when we feel as if our kids might have a less than perfect routine at their other parent's house. But the key to that last sentence is, it is how *we feel*.

Ultimately, our view of our child's other parent is likely somewhat biased, and not usually positively. Of course, we feel as if we are the only person on earth who knows what's best for our child. But so does your ex. If you aren't on the same page about what that 'best' looks like, and you can't peacefully find a middle ground to settle on, allow them to play out their version of 'best' at their home, and find your version for yours. Your children do thrive on routine, so make sure that they know what to expect in your home, rather than guessing what's going on in their other home and compensating. This again comes down to boundaries, which we'll talk about in just a minute.

If your child's other parent has abused you, navigating a co-parenting situation is not only difficult, but it can also be incredibly traumatic. In these cases, seek specialist help and advice if you are able to, from domestic abuse charities or a counsellor who specialises in this type of trauma recovery. Finding a support group of people who have been through the same or similar experiences to you that you can lean on is always a great idea if you can access one. The 'Own My Life' course can be a good way for women who have suffered domestic abuse to connect with other survivors and work towards overcoming their trauma, which is especially important if the cause of that trauma is now tethered to you via your child. Read on for expert advice on coping in these circumstances. If contact with your ex is traumatic, painful or difficult, you can communicate through a third party and even have that party facilitate handovers. Parallel parenting is probably going to be the option for you in this instance.

One other thing: you don't have to tell your co-parent that parallel parenting is the technique you're employing. They might be busy trying to enforce their 'best' on to you and asking you to stop being so strict with bedtime or telling you that you have to do extra hours on your child's reading. This is only proof that they *do* care about the kids, whether or not you agree with how they go about showing it.

They might not want to accept parallel parenting (if they're busy trying to get you to conform to their set-up), so in these cases, simply keep contact to a minimum, accept their criticism or advice with a simple 'Thank you for your thoughts on that' and then continue with your journey to be the best single parent you can be, making sure that your children have consistent parenting from you at home whenever they are with you.

Co-parenting

Co-parenting is the most common term for single parents who share custody with the children's other partner. This might be an even 50/50 split of time, or as little as a few hours every other week. However frequently (or infrequently) your child's other parent is in their life, finding a way to approach parenting as a team is always the best outcome for everyone involved, if that is possible. Sometimes it simply isn't, in which case you can skip back to the previous paragraph and work towards this one in your own time.

If you are able to manage communication with your children's other parent, you may be able to set things up so that your children have relatively consistent experiences at both their homes, however often they move between them. The truth is, there isn't a 'best' way to co-parent. Every child is different and every circumstance is too. The stereotype of children automatically going to their mum for the majority of the time and seeing dad every other weekend simply doesn't hold true any more. (However, nine out of ten single parents are women, so there are still a lot more women heading single-parent homes.)

More and more split families are dividing their time with the kids differently, predominantly because modern work schedules are shifting, and typically both parents have jobs to navigate alongside parenting. Although you don't have to work out immediately where the kids will spend most of their time, or how you'll split the week, if you are working with a co-parent, it is worth making this decision your key priority post-split. Once you set a precedent for how the children split their time and you settle into a routine that the children are happy with, it will not only be tough to uproot this and start from scratch, but legally things can get a little tricky too. If you decide to have your childcare set-up court-ordered, in order for either parent to request changes you'll have to go back to court. And even if you avoid legally setting out your custody arrangements, once you have a working set-up, the onus will be on the parent wanting change to prove that it is in the best interests of the children if the other parent disagrees and decides to go the legal route. Keeping an open line of communication between co-parents is the best way to navigate changes in circumstances in a conflict-free way.

Jamie Redknapp, former professional footballer and co-parent to two children, says: 'One of my biggest pieces of advice for successful co-parenting is, without a doubt, to put the children first. They need to be your number-one priority. It's also important to ensure that your children feel their parents are on the same page and working together as a team. It's not always easy to achieve this, but making an effort to try to make it work leads to happier, more settled children.'

As Jamie says, when you are making these decisions, keep your children's needs at the front of your mind, but be realistic about your needs too. It's unlikely both of you will have exactly the same idea about how you'd like the weekly time split to work, so be prepared to negotiate, and remember that this conversation isn't about winning an argument with your ex, it's about what will be best for the children. Yes, you might want them with you all day, every day, but you will need time to work, to sleep, to build your new life too. Once you have your time split decided on, try to keep things as regular as possible so that your children know what to expect and can find security in the familiar routine.

Remember, also, that however good your co-parenting relationship is, you get to make your own decisions about how you run your home, and how you parent your children when they are with you.

Control and letting go

'We can't control how someone else acts; we can only ever control how we interact, and react to what that person is doing,' says co-parenting advocate Aaron Dale (@raisingboys_2men). And he is absolutely right, so repeat after us: 'I cannot control my co-parent.' Now say it like you mean it! When it comes to our children, letting go of control is one of the biggest challenges there is. We want to wrap them up in cotton wool and protect them from the world around them. This can play out in attempting to control their surroundings (improbable) including their other parent (impossible).

Spending time and energy trying to control your co-parent and the way they do things is completely pointless. It's not only pointless, it is potentially damaging to your peace of mind and a waste of your precious time and resources. As parents, we give our children as much information as possible and equip them with tools to make the best decisions they can for themselves. Then we hold them when they make mistakes and give them room to grow. Doing the same with your co-parent will be much, much harder, but by letting go of any control of their life, or a perceived right to it, will give them the freedom they need to grow too. And their growth is good for them. (As is yours.)

Boundaries

Oh, the joy of boundaries! We speak about them a lot in this book. They're important in just about every area of life, but perhaps none more so than in your co-parenting relationship. Once you learn to maintain boundaries between yourself and your ex, you will have a chance at building a happy co-parenting team for your children. But putting boundaries in place and maintaining them with your ex is not easy, particularly if you are recovering from abuse.

Psychotherapist Charlotte Fox Weber, author of *What We Want*, says: 'Boundaries are everything, and rarely come naturally – especially when we're recovering from abuse.' She recommends keeping communication to a minimum in these circumstances, to help prevent boundaries being overstepped. 'I think it's essential to keep communication as efficient and unambiguous as possible if you're dealing with an abusive ex. Whenever possible, don't invite room for negotiation or further discussion, however tempting it might be at vulnerable moments. If you're co-parenting with an abusive ex and you still have tender and affectionate feelings for this person, it's important to protect yourself from further disappointment and surprise, and that sometimes means sticking to the agreement, even if you wish you could connect on a personal level.'

This is really important, and it means maintaining the boundaries on your side too; for example, you can't expect the other person to keep to strict handover timings and a rigid schedule if you want flexibility on your end to change arrangements when you have other plans. Keeping childcare arrangements to a fixed and regular schedule is one of the simplest boundaries for you both to set and maintain, from which other behavioural boundaries can follow suit. Charlotte says: 'Ordinary rules keep arrangements clear, and even if your ex is charming and persuasive occasionally, establishing basic arrangements will set up respectful guidelines. If you've been abused by this person, recalibrating standards goes a long way.'

The easiest way to maintain boundaries is to maintain space, and sometimes this means holding your tongue, no matter how hard that feels. 'It's always a good idea to aim for respect going both ways, and as tempting as it might be to hurl vitriol at a vile ex, you want to protect yourself from flying off the handle,' says Charlotte. 'Minimal communication is usually optimal if you're dealing with someone abusive. You're not likely to get through to the person by going into detail and engaging in endless back and forth. I do think that mediation and therapy can be helpful for difficult conversations.'

It is important to remember that although you can't control someone trying to overstep your boundaries, you *can* control how strictly you enforce them. If your co-parent isn't willing to be respectful, using a mediator or cutting off direct contact altogether might be necessary.

Finances

The single biggest point of conflict between co-parents is money (and we will talk more about finances in Chapter 4). The best way around this is to work towards achieving complete financial independence from your co-parent (whether or not you should have to) so that you are not reliant on their contributions to survive, or thrive, as a single parent. Unfortunately, with financial dependence comes control, and many co-parents use money as a weapon when it comes to navigating the parenting minefield. Having said this, sometimes it is simply not possible to achieve financial independence from your co-parent, especially in the early days of single parenting (although you may have more of an idea of how you will achieve it once you've read Chapter 4, on finances).

We spoke to co-parenting advocate Aaron Dale (@raisingboys_2men) about getting comfortable with child-support payments. Although he uses gendered language referring to the dad as the provider and mum as recipient of support payments, the same logic can be applied to whoever has primary custody of the children and the other parent as the financial contributor. 'As a single parent, you're doing so much work, and you need that financial support.' He says it is important to remember that: 'We're not paying for our child. So many people have that mindset, but you're not, you're paying to support the upbringing of your child. From the woman's point of view, it's an entitlement. If you are unable to come to an agreement with the dad, go to the Child Maintenance Service (CMS). Don't feel ashamed about it. It's an entitlement.

'Removing shame from the financial requirements of raising a child is vital. Unfortunately, our economic system is often not equipped to support single-parent families.'

On the other hand, Aaron stresses: 'Don't use money as a weapon. Because it's one of the only cards we have in reality. And just because you're able to dodge the system because the CMS is flawed, there are ways around it, don't [sic]. Just because you're able to, that's not a victory for you, that's a defeat for your child.'

Having a realistic view of what child-support payments are for is also important, especially if you are the contributing parent. Aaron says: 'I've got friends that have spent £150 on a pair of trainers for their child. Not being mindful that the mum actually needs gas and electric payments, that there's not actually that much food in the house. So you come along and you think, "Oh, look how good a dad I am. My child's got £150 trainers." But what that household needs, including your child, is to make sure the bills are being paid and there's food in the cupboards. Your co-parent receiving money is an entitlement and a need, not a want.'

Of course, making your co-parent see things this way can be challenging, although tearing these pages out, highlighting them, and posting them through the letterbox is an option.

Confidence

Operating as a lone head of a household is a lot of pressure and, like most important roles in life, confidence is key. When you're operating alongside a co-parent, it can add pressure. It's as if you're a regional manager and the other local branch is always trying to prove to the CEO (your child, in this instance) that their branch is better, more efficient and decidedly more fun. But putting the power to judge your branch's performance in your co-manager's hands (or the highly bribable CEO's) is a big mistake.

The key to parenting success is confidence, and nothing makes co-parenting easier than genuinely believing that you're doing a good job at home. This can be extra challenging if you have a difficult relationship with your co-parent, particularly if they were abusive. Charlotte Fox Weber says: 'Recovering from abuse requires bolstering the validity of your perspective. You may have second-guessed yourself for years, and you might continue to doubt your own point of view, so finding nurture and support goes a long way.'

If you struggle to find that confidence from within, look for people who will help to bolster it from outside. 'Find a select few who get it, who love you and care and can hold space for the twists and turns of what you're dealing with,' says Charlotte. 'If you're porous to other people's opinions, it's really important to be discerning about who weighs in, and well-meaning friends and family can still get it spectacularly wrong. Don't feel obligated to update everyone about everything: keeping people informed should be for your benefit.'

Remember that you are the narrator of your story.

'You can give the elevator pitch one-liner if you want people to know the basic facts of whatever is happening, but it's up to you if you feel like going into detail about your situation,' says Charlotte.

'It can be exhausting and unhelpful to feel pressured to inform all your friends about your life, especially if friends are insensitive and say callous things that make you feel bad. I often say to people in a crisis: beware of unworthy authority. People can say clumsy and clichéd things without understanding the impact and without having insight about your experience, and it's really important to protect yourself from the injuries of misattuned people weighing in. Beware of unworthy authority and recognise your own limitations as well. When you trust a therapist or lawyer or specialist to guide you with something, allow for help. Resistance and isolation are dangerous when recovering from abuse and it's a wonderful relief to let people help. Allow people to support you.'

Finding a group that have had a similar experience to you and are also navigating co-parenting with an abusive ex can be an enormous help. Charlotte says, 'Group support can be a tonic. It's often astonishing and encouraging to realise that you're not the only one to go through hell. Others have emerged from the despair you feel, and you might also discover that you've come a long way when you see someone struggling with an issue you've worked through. A crisis can sever ties with some people in your life but makes space for new connections too. Cracks are where the light comes in. If you feel fragmented, overwrought, undone by the change in your circumstances, joining or creating a group can be bolstering in myriad ways. A cohesive group can hold and facilitate growth in beautiful ways.'

Emotions

Trying to keep emotions out of co-parenting is like trying to shave your legs with a bread knife: painful and ineffective; however, letting your emotions rule your co-parenting would be like trying to use the bread knife to shave your chin: downright dangerous. The fact is, very few people choose their co-parent. At least, if they knew they were going to be in a co-parenting situation, this wouldn't have been the person they would have chosen.

Many, many co-parents are arriving at this juncture as a result of one or more traumatic events: abuse, adultery, abandonment or the breakdown of a relationship. These are emotional situations, and your emotions towards your co-parent and surrounding the events that led you here are completely valid and important; however, they are separate from your co-parenting situation. If you can keep them separate from co-parenting, you are giving your kids the best chance possible at having a happy and secure life in both their homes.

Keep your emotions towards your co-parent away from your children. It is hard. Oh man, is it hard? It is hard to hear your child cry for their other parent, when they've failed to show up for them. It is hard hearing your child idolise a co-parent that abused you and isolated you from friends and family. It is hard seeing your child away on holiday having a great time with your ex and the person they cheated on you with and left you for. But these things are hard for you, not for your child.

Keep these hardships away from your children. Keep these emotions away from your children. Don't keep them away from yourself, allow yourself to feel them, and seek support from friends and family, because having an outlet for all the stresses of co-parenting is essential. Creating a 'neutral' emotion to convey to your child about your co-parent can be really useful. (It also gives you the chance for a little amateur dramatics, if you've ever fancied yourself as an actor. You've just been cast as 'co-parent who feels totally and completely neutral towards a former lover/cheating ex/abusive partner and manages to witness any number of bonkers behaviours from them towards the child that they treasure more than any earthly being and remain cool, calm and collected. *Action!*)

Practise maintaining a neutral emotional space for your child to explore their own emotional reactions to their other parent with you, whether positive or negative. If they are excited and happy about something they've done with their co-parent, respond with 'That's great!' and centre their emotions, not yours. Likewise, if your co-parent lets them down, or upsets them, and they are sad and frustrated, comfort them and acknowledge their feelings without adding yours into the mix. Phrases like 'This must be so hard for you' will validate their feelings and create a space for them to share with you without worrying how it will make you feel, or suggesting to them that you are against their co-parent, or feeling anything other than fine. Because you are, of course, fine. (Remember that episode of *Friends* where Ross is 'fine'? That's how fine you are.)

Actually being fine

Although acting 'I'm fine' well is a great coping mechanism, how great would actually being fine feel? Very, very good. If you want to really work through your issues and get to a place of contentment, therapy can be especially helpful. Charlotte Fox Weber makes a case for the healing powers of facing the demons within.

'Therapy allows for safe exploration. It's supportive but it can also be challenging and expansive, adjusting perspectives and opening new healthier ways of relating. If you feel threadbare and insecure, it can help validate emotional injuries which have never been acknowledged. Therapy holds space for self-discovery and growth. The pace and process can be idiosyncratic and personal to what works for you, and speaking your mind is harder than it sounds. There are layers of performance and defensiveness in so many areas of life and one of the luxuries of therapy is that it's possible to be unvarnished and bold in digging deep. You can face yourself without flinching. When you've experienced trauma, there are fragments and memories and associations and beliefs which might be scattered across your life, and making sense of situations allows for a coherent narrative. Therapy can help you understand yourself and find ease, however stressful the circumstances. Whether you're in the midst of a crisis or you're reflecting on a crisis from decades ago, it's never too late to sort through issues and find new possibilities.'

Private therapy might not be accessible to all, but you can

speak to your healthcare provider about options for financial aid or complementary treatments, and many charities provide access to therapy, particularly for survivors of abuse.

Keep your nose out

One way to minimise emotions getting in the way of your co-parenting relationship is to try and know the absolute minimum about what your children's other parent is getting up to. If it doesn't directly impact your child, it shouldn't interest you. The first step in this is having a clear definition of where your role as a parent begins and ends. Aaron Dale (@raisingboys_2men) simplifies what this means for co-parents: 'Both parents should be coming to the table knowing they're doing their part, that's seeing the kids on a regular basis, that's being consistent in paying money [if that is their role]. That's one battle won, no one can complain now, because your child is good. It's both people not focusing on what the other person is doing and making sure you're doing your part.'

Step one, then, is understanding your parenting responsibility, and the second part is minding your own business when it comes to your co-parent's. Aaron says: 'It's staying out of [their] world, and [them] staying out of your world. When you were together in that relationship, you were entitled to know about each other's world. It's understanding that that relationship's broken down. So those entitlements are no longer there.' It is when you start asking questions that there is room for conflict, explains Aaron: 'Where were you? Where did you go? Who was that man? Who was that woman? That's no longer your concern, so stay out of each other's worlds.'

How do you do that? Go back and re-read our section on boundaries (on page 53) if you need to.

Communication

Communication with your children's other parent is the key to whether you have a good or a bad co-parenting relationship. There isn't necessarily a right or a wrong way for co-parents to talk, but there is a right and a wrong way for *you* in your personal situation. The key is to work out what that is, to allow your co-parent to figure out what theirs is, and to try to find the common ground in the middle. This carries on from the boundaries we have just discussed. If communication with your ex is emotionally triggering for you, set boundaries around how and when you have to speak to them, and stick to those boundaries. Remember that any rules you make will need to work both ways; for example, if you don't want your ex to communicate with you when your kids are in your care, you will have to accept them making the same rule for you, so you may not be able to speak to the kids when it's their other parent's turn to have them stay. Some single parents prefer to have conversations over text or email so that there is a written log of exchanges, but while you're building your mountain of evidence for every time your co-parent forgets to take them to a party, or fails to bring them back an hour earlier (as 'clearly promised via this text message'), consider what you're planning to do with this evidence.

Many co-parents get wrapped up in the narrative of better vs worse parent, and lose sight of the bigger picture. Do you want to be right, or happy? Sometimes you can't be both. If your co-parent constantly forgets things, even things you've messaged them to pre-warn or remind them of, you'll have to decide whether to bite the bullet and manage their time, send that extra 30-minute warning text from afar, or relinquish control and just realise that as long as the kids are OK you might be the only one that is being impacted by the lateness, or the forgetfulness. Being right about being the better parent, about following the rules, about every darn thing there is to be right about, doesn't mean anything if it's getting in the way of you being happy, and the happiness of your kids.

This consideration plays into your communication with your co-parent, too. The biggest piece of advice we can give you here is to avoid replying in haste. Unless there is an emergency that needs urgent action, take a moment before replying to their messages. A five-minute rule is usually a good rule of thumb, and learning a few mindfulness techniques will help you get the best outcome from these exchanges too.

Firstly, rather than letting your emotional reactions guide your response, observe the emotional response itself. Do you feel anxious? Stressed? Angry? Sad? Think about why the message has made you feel that way. Before you write your reply, think firstly whether you need to reply at all. Could you acknowledge without furthering the conversation? Is the situation resolvable? Once your emotional reaction has evaporated and you're working on a reply (if needed), keep in mind the rule about being right, or being happy. The goal is the happiness of our kids and our own happiness. Our goal should be keeping the peace and obtaining an outcome that is best for ourselves and our children. So let them be right, if that is what they are aiming for, and just pick your battles at the times when it matters for maintaining your peace.

Helen Thorn, author of *Get Divorced, Be Happy*, says: 'I'd advise not replying to text messages, or emails straight away. Someone used to say to me, don't reply (unless it's an emergency, obviously), but sit on it, because I'd be wanting to write back in sweary capital letters! Have a trusted friend, who you can release the rage onto, every time you have an interaction with your ex. And know that being angry is OK.'

Enforcing boundaries (we just covered those, remember?) with your communication is something that can work really well, too. Helen told us: 'We have established a weekly phone call, in which we both have to have a list of things that we need to discuss, whether it's sports, PE, whatever; it's very businesslike.' Limiting interaction time can really help, too. 'Make drop-offs and pick up really quick, have everything ready,' says Helen. 'I like having all the bags at the front door and I kind of step back. It's inevitable, especially if you've got primary-aged children that you will be in the same room with them. If you're at a school play, you can sit on the opposite side of the room and say, I'm going to be sitting in the front row or I'll be in the back row and I'll be more comfortable if I'm not near you.'

If communication is a challenge, you can either use mediation services or even limit interactions to an app. Kate Daly is the co-founder of Amicable, the couples online divorce service, and recommends working towards a less intimate relationship to find co-parenting success: 'Working with a specially trained divorce or co-parenting coach can really help you stay on track, and we all behave better with someone else in the room so don't underestimate how far you can travel with the right kind of support. If you need a bit of distance between you then why not try one of the co-parenting apps on the market. Our amicable co-parenting app has suggested goals and different "lives with" patterns to suit kids of different ages and stages. Giving some thought to and becoming more skilled at creating a good working co-parenting relationship will pay dividends and it's not something we tend to think of in the maelstrom of a separation. But a bit of time invested and the observation of some boundaries and getting the relationship onto a less "intimate" footing can help.'

The grey rock method

One more thing about communication: for those who have to co-parent with an abuser or toxic ex, maintaining contact as a necessity might be especially hard, and communication may remain a trigger for anxiety or stress, no matter how much time passes post-split. Your ex might try to overstep the mark with communication in these instances, because they will be unwilling to relinquish control, and it is important to remember that you do not have to communicate with them just because they are your child's other parent. You can state to them that you wish to communicate with them only about their child's direct needs. If they continue to ignore this you can take steps to stop them contacting you, or request that all communication takes place via a third party.

Many people employ something called the 'grey rock method' when communicating with a difficult ex, which essentially involves mimicking a grey rock whenever you encounter them. Make yourself completely immovable, uninteresting, personality-less and bland. Reply with simple yes, no, thank you, OK messages and do not engage with personal questions. When they ask what you're up to, say 'nothing' or 'working'. The aim is that they will get no pleasure from trying to engage with a grey rock, and will eventually move on and stop trying. In an ideal world, they will learn to separate you from the child you share, and you will be able to do the same in turn.

Charlotte Fox Weber says: 'The grey rock method is brilliant for sparing you the energy of trying to explain nuance and justify and reiterate each and every issue. Allow yourself the joyous freedom of conversational laziness. Rather than feeling pulled in to talk through each and every thing, you can make a point concisely and stick to that point, repeating it when necessary. Remind yourself that you don't have to charm or convince your ex in any way. You don't have to dazzle. In fact, it's a luxury to be boring and give less conversationally. Let's say your ex tries to get you to dog-sit and you're uncomfortable taking the dog. You say no once, and your ex asks again. 'As I said before, I'm not going to take your dog,' you say. If your ex asks you why, you don't need to explain. Just repeat what you've already said, and leave it at that. You do not need to prove yourself further or go into detail about how much you love dogs, but how on this particular occasion, you can't take the dog. Keep it simple and ordinary. Co-parenting doesn't mean you have to accommodate and bend over backwards for every particularity.'

Remember that perfecting the grey rock method takes practice, especially when dealing with someone who triggers you emotionally.

Holidays

Splitting holidays with your co-parent can be tricky, but it can also be a game-changer in terms of single-parent life balance. Seeing your child away on a holiday without you can absolutely break your heart; however, if you can time a holiday for the same time with your best friends in Ibiza or a Butlin's weekender, the child-free time can be the ultimate parenting recharge to unwind and reclaim a little slice of yourself. The key to this is, again, about establishing a good routine and communication with your children's other parent, and trying to be routine in how your children's time is split.

There is no one-size-fits-all approach, but you could establish rules such as deciding at the start of the year who will have the kids for which half-term, how you'll split any big holidays you celebrate like Easter or Christmas, Diwali, Yom Kippur, Eid al-Adha, bank holidays, and when you are planning to take trips that will require changes to childcare routines. Some co-parenting teams will be fine with adhoc changes – many won't. The fact is, you'll face some big family dates without your kids. If you have a co-parent, one of you will likely need to be away from the children at difficult times (like birthdays, Mother's or Father's Day and so on). If you can all spend the days together, great, but if you can't, making plans for how you'll cope on these days is a good idea.

Many single parents club together at these times and look after each other. The beauty of having single-parent friends in the same situation as you is that they just 'get it'. Find friends that will spend Christmas Day with you in pyjamas sans kids, doing karaoke and drinking champagne. And move Christmas Day with the kids to the day you get them back. You both get two Christmases, and everyone's a winner.

Step-parents and bonus parents

One or both of you might move on at some point and get new partners. Having a conversation as early as possible with your co-parent about how you plan to approach this will avoid heartache further down the line. In an ideal world, you'll have a plan for how and when you might introduce your kids to a new partner, and your co-parent will be on the same page. It's never nice to find out about an ex's new partner via your child, but unfortunately it happens. If it happens to you, try to take that five-minute rule before you display any reactions. If you're angry, it might be valid, but perhaps you're actually just hurt and sad. We'll return again to the point we discussed earlier about letting go of control. At the end of the day, you can't control how your co-parent chooses to conduct their dating life; it simply isn't your business any more.

The only reason for you to get involved is if you have concerns regarding the safety of your child, so unless you have reasons to raise concerns with your co-parent for any reason other than this, try very hard to live and let live. As long as your children are safe and happy, that is all that matters. It can also be tempting to try to extract information about your co-parent's new relationship or love life from your child – do not do this either. Our job is to provide our children with love and safety when they are in our care. They do not have to pay for this service with anything, and they certainly do not have to provide you with reassurance or show 'loyalty' by eschewing the offers of love from their co-parent or new partners that are brought into their lives. The more love our children have, the better. The more people who love them, the better.

You might be predisposed to disapprove of your co-parent's new partners, but if they love your kids, they will be bringing something positive into their lives, and one day you might be able to love them for it. If the thought of them having a step-parent is stressing you out, try rebranding to 'bonus parent'. Because having more people to watch over them is a bonus.

Aaron (@raisingboys_2men) says: 'That seems to be one

of the biggest things men come to me about: having another man around their child and their child's mum moving on. My child has a stepdad. But that doesn't change my role as dad. And I think a lot of us worry sometimes that someone else coming in is going to mean our role changes. And our role never changes. We just have to continue to do our role. And I think it's so important: just because someone else is in mum's life, or someone else is in dad's life, we still play our role, the same way we would have before.'

The grey spaces

The separation of parents usually happens for big reasons. It tends to take a lot for people to decide to separate from the other parent of their children, especially when they then intend to, or have to, co-parent with that person. Whether you are the initiator of the split, or it has been forced upon you, it is likely that in the short term you will need to see things in black and white in order to cope. This usually means seeing your ex, your co-parent, as mostly bad. It is easier to com-partmentalise your ex as 'bad' to give you the strength you need to move forward at this very tough moment in your life. If you've made the decision to leave an abusive ex, it will be easier to find the strength to do so, and move forward, if you paint them as completely 'bad'. If your ex has cheated on you, the same applies. Even if you've cheated on them, remembering the 'bad' things they did that led you to stray is inevitable and understandable. They may need to remain the 'bad' one for a number of months or even years while you find your feet, and this is where the bulk of co-parenting challenges and conflicts will arise.

It can sometimes feel impossible to separate the need to

get over your ex and move forward with your life from the need to amicably co-parent with them. Give yourself a break for this completely understandable black-and-white thinking. But be ready to recognise, and make space for, the grey: the moment that your ex treats you with compassion or doesn't pull you up for making a mistake; the moment that they don't make a big deal about the fact that you've forgotten the shin pads, but simply turns up with spares; when they show up for you emotionally because they care about you as their baby's other parent, not because there is something in it for them; when you allow yourself to see your co-parent for all their shades of grey (not those kinds – it's your ex, ick), you'll feel enormously grateful that your child's other parent isn't a monster after all, but a flawed human, just like you. They're not perfect, but your black-and-white view of them is subject to shifting and cracking. The cracks are where the light gets in. And seeing the good in them allows you to hope that those are the parts they're passing on to your child.

The rollercoaster

As with every other element of single-parent life, it's important to remember that your co-parenting relationship is subject to change. Things might start hard and get easier. They might start smoothly and get rockier. Your co-parenting relationship might be a rollercoaster of highs, lows, rocky patches, loop the loops (or going round in never-ending circles of frustration), some large periods of reversing and some glorious ascents. As with all parenting, things are not linear. This too shall pass. You might think you've found a good rhythm with co-parenting, or that you have finally settled on a routine that works, when one of you then gets a new job, or finds a new partner, or decides that they need to move home, and so on, and everything is thrown up in the air again. There will be sicknesses to navigate, family crises, disagreements and change.

Setting strong boundaries and having fall-back plans, support networks and strong self-care routines to cope in these times is vital. Seeking legal advice where needed can be enormously reassuring, and free advice services and charities can also help if you can't afford private help in this area.

The rollercoaster of co-parenting might not be the ride you signed up for with your children's other parent when you met them, but you're on it now, so buckle up (and prepare for the possibility of vomiting).

My single-parent story

Aaron Dale, co-parent and founder of Raising Boys To Men and @raisingboys_2men on Instagram

I was raised by a single mum, and actually grew up on the same estate as my dad and his other family. So my dad wasn't really in my life, but he was *visibly* in my life. He came back into my life, then left it again, he was very inconsistent. I didn't really have a good example of manhood, fatherhood or anything like that. I got into a relationship with my eldest son's mum when I was about 20 or 21. It wasn't the greatest relationship and I don't think there was any longevity in it, but she fell pregnant and we weren't able to make it work. I navigated that situation quite immaturely; I was still learning about myself, and learning about manhood. And then I met my youngest's mum about two years later. We were together for about four or five years. She fell pregnant, and again that didn't quite work out. The first time – I hold my hands up – I made a lot of mistakes. So the second time, I decided that this is going to be a much better situation. And it turned out to be. My youngest now has a stepdad and I think that's a beautiful thing. I feel like I have two completely different relationships with each woman, and I co-parent very differently with both of them. But I would say that the children are happy in both situations, and that's the main thing.

Aaron's advice for co-parents

Make sure you're doing your part. Both people are coming to the table, knowing that they're both doing their part, seeing the kids on a regular basis and/or being consistent with paying money. That's one battle won, no one can really complain now, because our child is good.

And don't feel that you have to put on an act for your child. Sometimes we want, or we need, to do things together, we feel the need to be a family. You're creating a facade for the child, which when another person comes into the mix, or mum moves on or dad moves on, that whole dynamic has to break. Sometimes we try to protect our children so much that we don't want them to go through any pain. We don't want them to see anything negative, we don't want them to go through trauma, but we can actually make things worse. We need to say: 'Look, mummy and daddy aren't together. This is how it is. But we're going to walk you through this pain. We're going to be here to support you through this pain.'

3

Finding Mrs Doubtfire – Childcare Arrangements

Every single-parent family set-up is different, but one thing is true across the board: it takes a village to raise a child. Some villages are, admittedly, smaller than others. You might be feeling as if you're currently in the world's smallest village, made up solely of you and your dependants, but if you try to do it all yourself, you're going to burn out. (Of course, you might actually *want* some residents of your village to move out.) The childcare solutions we discuss in this chapter are not exclusive to single parenting, and you may already have a great set-up in place, but when it comes to help and support, the more the merrier.

Having a co-parent to share childcare with doesn't necessarily make things easier (exes, right?) and building a good co-parenting relationship with someone with whom there are very real reasons for you to have split, permanently, is not easy. Meanwhile for solo parents, some have parents, aunts, cousins and friends within a stone's throw to help out, whereas others are going it completely alone on different continents from their families. Whatever your set-up, finding the right childcare for you is an absolute game changer. But where do you start? In this chapter we are going to guide you through some of the main considerations when it comes to childcare, from the absolute basics of 'Where will my children be while I work?' to 'How will I ever go on a date again?'

Whether or not you have sole parental responsibility (that is, full custody), there will be times when they are in your care when you need them to, well, not be. Your children's childcare needs evolve almost as quickly as your children do, so finding something perfect right away isn't necessary, but finding something functional is. You might need childcare so that you can go to work (although finding a job that will pay you enough to cover the cost is another challenge; our work and finances chapters lay ahead). You might need childcare so that you have time to study. You might need childcare so that you have time to run errands, attempt to reboot your social life, or simply so that you have the time and space to breathe. The most important thing is finding somewhere consistent, where you know your child is happy and safe, with someone you can trust. It *is* possible, we promise. Here we'll run through the main childcare settings so that you can think about what might be right for your children, whatever ages or stages they're at. You might already have a working childcare set-up in place, in which case you can put a pin in this chapter until it needs to change for any reason. And if you're the parent of children old enough to leave at home on their own, you might want to skip over this chapter altogether, or pop to your nearest cafe to read it in peace with a coffee and a slice of cake.

Nannies

A nanny is someone who provides care for your children in a private setting, usually your own house. Whereas childminders or shared childcare set-ups operate in another location with multiple children in one setting and sets hours of business, a nanny tends to work around your schedule, providing flexible childcare and assistance to allow you to work, or get out and about for other aspects of life. A nanny doesn't necessarily have to be employed full-time by one family, some families will share the cost of a nanny and have help on different days, or they find an arrangement where their needs match and childcare responsibilities can be shared.

Professional nannies may have specialist qualifications, and enhanced safety checks and insurances, but not all will, so make sure you do your research, and if you can use a trusted recommendation to find your perfect nanny, then do so. There are some enormous positives to finding a nanny, which include more flexibility for you (around non-flexible work set-ups), allowing you to build a work and home life that works for your new single-parent status, even acting as a safety net for when your child is ill. If you have a co-parent, you may be able to split costs and use the same nanny so that your children have a stable childcare set-up at both homes.

This stability will be enhanced the longer your kids have the same nanny in their lives, and many find that working with a nanny is akin to a co-parent in terms of shared childcare and logistical responsibility. This shared responsibility, flexibility and dependability tends to come at a premium, however, and nannies tend to be out of budget for many single or solo parents that are shouldering the cost of childcare alone.

Au pairs

An au pair is similar to a nanny, in that they can provide private, flexible childcare support for your family, but rather than being an employee that comes and goes around working hours (albeit flexible ones), an au pair will become a temporary part of the family, living in your home and helping out with the children along with assisting with the day-to-day running of the house. Since you will be hosting and supporting this individual, you will pay them considerably lower wages, as their bed and board is a part of their salary. This set-up works well for many families, but it is worth noting that an au pair typically stays for between three and twelve months, so it isn't a long-term solution, but it might be an option if you are finding your feet and think that adding someone else into the mix might be a help, rather than a hindrance.

Childminders

Professional childminders typically provide affordable childcare in a private, group setting, often at their own homes. They should have the relevant safety checks in place, which you should ask any prospective childminder to provide you with proof of during the interview process. Finding a nearby childminder can be like gold-dust, since not only will your child have somewhere safe and dependable to be when you're working or busy, but they'll also probably have a ready-made friendship group with the other children they spend their days with.

As they grow older, their childminder may be able to be their school wraparound carer, doing school drop-offs and pick-ups, and even providing ad hoc childcare or babysitting when needed.

Nursery

Private nurseries tend to accept children from around their first birthday (some will accept children younger, but generally not younger than six months). The majority of children that attend nursery start between the age of one and two years. Some nurseries are oversubscribed, and have long waiting lists in operation, so many new parents add their children to these lists before they are even born.

Most nurseries are vetted by services such as Ofsted, so you can look up their latest reports and scores online to help make your decision, but getting in and seeing the nursery is really the only way to know if you can picture your child being happy in a given setting.

One advantage of a good nursery setting is that it will provide structured and dependable childcare (for example, if a nanny or childminder is sick, you're left without childcare, whereas a staff team is often able to cover absences) that also runs during school holidays. Furthermore, if you have an only child, as a single parent a nursery setting will give your child access to a social network of children their own age for them to start forming bonds and connections with their peers. Drawbacks include the rigidity of the timings (being late for pick-ups often carries hefty fines) and costs, which are sky-high and showing no signs of coming down at the time of writing. There is often a minimum number of days that your child will be are required to attend the nursery in order for you to secure a place, although some parents are able to opt for one or two days of formal childcare, such as a nursery, and one or two days of a more casual arrangement such as family help.

Family help

Childcare set-ups tend to fall into one of two categories: formal and informal. The former tend to be the ones you pay for or that are managed by the state (such as educational settings), whereas the latter are undertaken by the people in your life – often your relatives, or your child's relatives.

For some people that become single parents, immediately relocating to be close to their family is a no-brainer. For primary or sole carers of particularly young children this is even more popular, since the child or children don't have established (or well established) routines or networks in any given location, and making the move to be closer to your family so that you have help on hand just makes sense for all of you. If, conversely, you live close to your child's other parent's family, consider whether they will be there to help you in the future. Remember that aside from their relationship with you, they have one with your children, so you might be surprised at how willing they are to slot into your regular childcare schedule.

Family childcare holds many advantages: first and foremost, it is often free. Not only will your parents be happy to help with school runs if they're able, but they'll also probably provide the kids with a delicious home-cooked meal that you can also enjoy a portion of when you arrive for handover (or at the very least a cuppa and a chocolate biscuit). The flexibility of having help on hand when you're stuck in a meeting or run into transport issues is invaluable, akin to having a partner or co-parent to lean on in a crisis, and your child will benefit from having other family figures they can lean on and be loved by regularly, too. On the other hand, the flexibility of this childcare set-up will run both ways, and you'll need to remember that your family members have lives of their own too. When they're off on holidays, unwell or simply have other plans, you'll have childcare gaps to fill that might be tricky if you don't usually utilise more formal childcare settings. For this reason, many single parents that live close to family prefer to divide between family and formal settings for their childcare (if budgets allow), not only so that they have a fall-back for add-ons if family are unavailable, but so that their children have the social and educational benefits of the formal childcare, too. Having said that, nothing beats having a sibling or parent closeby to offload your problems or your child (or both) when you need a break, and those relationships are to be treasured if you are blessed with them.

We'd also like to add that it is, once again, a failing of state systems that forces so many parents, both single and non-single, to turn to family members to fill the childcare gaps in their lives for financial reasons. The lack of affordable childcare often means that grandparents are essentially being forced back into the (unpaid) labour market once retired to contribute to the care of their grandchildren. While it is undeniably wonderful that so many children have close relationships with their grandparents, it would be better if the time they spent together was a choice, and not a necessity. Try to remove expectations from the requests you're making of family, particularly elderly family members. They will probably want to help, but they're also likely to be even more tired of this broken system that makes single parenting such a challenge, having existed in it for longer. You should also remember that retired grandparents get tired very quickly when looking after young children. It's easy to assume that because they seem energetic or youthful they have the same energy levels as yourself.

Babysitters

Just like finding a nanny that the kids love, finding a reliable babysitter can be a game-changer. As with any other non-formal setting, safety, both of your child and their babysitter, should be the top priority. There are an increasing number of apps and services that offer flexible, accessible babysitting at short notice. If you're using a professional babysitting service or an app, make sure you know exactly what qualifications, experience and safety checks all babysitters go through before being able to take jobs. Where possible, use babysitters that you know, that your children are familiar with, and that you've had a recommendation for. But even if they tick all these boxes, you can still ask them to complete a basic DBS (or international equivalent) check and/or ask about their previous experience.

Many professional nursery staff do babysitting work on the side, so it may be worth asking your child's key worker if they are available for extra childcare shifts. Of course, people have been paying teenage neighbours, friends' kids and younger family members to look after their children for a few hours for decades. Find a set-up that works for you and build up to longer periods away to ensure all involved are comfortable with the set-up. Being away from your kids or leaving them with someone new for the first, second or third time is always stressful. Start small with a trip to the dentist or a coffee round the corner with a friend and check in with both your babysitter and your children to see how it went. Once you have a regular babysitter you'll be able to reclaim a little of your independence and make plans in the outside world again – if you want to, of course.

Pre-school

If you're living in the UK, once your child hits three, they will be eligible for some free childcare. This is different from country to country. If they are happy in a nursery or childminder setting, you can use your hours towards this cost, but at this age they can also attend a state pre-school, which are more closely controlled in terms of staffing, curriculum and opening hours. Opening hours tend to align with school hours, around 9am until 3pm, which can be a good opportunity to start easing yourself into school life without the rigidity of mandated attendance, if that fits with your work schedule, of course. It can also be a good way to ease your child into school life over the course of a couple of years. They may even continue onwards with the same peers to further ease their transition to school.

Although fees are subsidised or covered for working parents, part-time attendance or attendance for non-earning parents is chargeable, as is wraparound care or additional hours, so there may still be some costs involved. Attendance is much less strict than at school, though, so you can still make the most of term-time holiday prices and take ad hoc days off. The flipside of this is that a school timetable means that many pre-schools completely shut down during the school holidays, leaving you without childcare for multiple weeks a year.

Educational settings

Bless our schools. Bless our teachers. Bless our children's lunch staff, lollypop people, teaching assistants and all the other support staff. If you find a school that you love, that your child loves and that is easy for you to get to and from, life will be instantly sweeter. If you're coming into single parenthood once your children are already established in schools they love, you will have one less thing to worry about, but for all the new single parents with pre-school-age kids, please know that school starting age is a real turning point in terms of single parenthood. Yes, there are additional things to think about, to juggle, to remember and timings to figure out, but between the hours of roughly 8.30am and 3pm, five days a week, your child or children will be in safe hands, soaking up knowledge, being nurtured and cared for, and you will be completely free to focus on yourself.

When you're looking for this school, there are some additional things you might want to think about as a single parent, aside from the usual things such as school performance and the feel you get from the institution and staff when visiting. Firstly, if your child's other parent is still on the scene and you have shared parental responsibility, they will need to sign off on the school you child attends. Picking the school that is closest to you, but miles from them, or vice versa, is nonsensical if you'll be sharing pick-ups and drop-offs. If you have majority custody but they still share parental responsibility, involving them in the process of choosing a school may save a lot of headaches further down the line if they decide they disagree.

The second thing to consider is how easy the school run will be with just you to do it. If you can find a good school within walking distance, do it. Not only is the school run a great way to work some exercise and fresh air into both your daily routines, but the walk together will quickly become one of the highlights of your day (and theirs too). In addition, as they grow older they might be able to walk to and from school with friends without you going mad with worry. Being within walking distance of school will also mean that they'll likely have school peers within easy reach and they can build up a social circle and you can build up a school parent network of your own to depend upon.

Finally, check out the school's wraparound childcare options and clubs offerings. If they are under-resourced and oversubscribed you'll need to find additional childcare to cover the hours you need, which might leave you juggling options again.

Wraparound care

Most schools offer wraparound care in the form of breakfast and after-school clubs, which are usually relatively low in cost and dependable for childcare that lasts an entire 8am to 6pm working day. Since these clubs are run by the school, you can drop your child off, safe in the knowledge that they will be in the same building with the same people all day. They'll also probably be in the club with a few of their friends, and will be happy, and may even make a head start on their homework.

If you have to rely on these clubs every day, try not to feel guilty. There will be other children there frequently too, as not everyone is blessed with flexible working hours or under-standing bosses, whether single parent or not. Many kids start at school lamenting the extra hours and arriving home exhausted, but within a few months, and after establishing friendships (often with children from other years – great for social standing) at the clubs, they'll be begging you to sign up for extra days. Too late: the space will be gone, which brings us to the major downside of these wraparound clubs, depend-ing on the school, space may be limited and there is often a waiting list in operation. We'd recommend joining it as soon as you get a space secured at the school if you think you might need access to the club. And if you need to, you can always find a childminder in the interim. Or ask for flexible working (we'll address this on page 123) until a space frees up.

Clubs and activities

As your children get older, they will broaden their horizons with new activities and extra interests. These come with possibilities for new childcare settings (or, at the very least, snatches of free time). Some schools run great arrays of after-school activity clubs, which will buy you an extra hour or so after school, but it's worth checking out what's happening in the local area and figuring out what will be easy to get to, inexpensive and fun for your kids.

If you're self-employed, the precious hour or two of a club or lesson means catching up on emails, having a client meeting in the car, or organising your diary for the week. Alternatively, it might mean reading a book for an hour, something you'd never justify investing time in at home, with so much to be done, or meditating with noise-cancelling headphones at a warm poolside cafe while the kids learn to swim. Any time someone else is responsible for your child's safety, however brief, is time you can free your mind and have a mini break from the exhausting task of single parenting, and however you choose to use it, even if it's to doom-scroll on your phone or stare at a sports hall wall, is valid.

School holidays

Once the kids are in school, they have roughly three months a year off on school holidays. Since most workplaces offer just over a month of paid leave, this leaves you with quite a short-fall to cover as a single parent. Of course, this is a problem that all working parents face, and if you have a co-parent you may be able to split the load, but this still might leave a short-fall. If you have access to flexible working, you may be able to work from home or shift your working hours to accommodate having the kids at home more in the school holidays, but if you can't you'll need to cover these hours somehow. There is an endless variety of school holiday clubs that your children can try out, and they vary wildly in terms of activity and price. Some are play-based settings that are essentially grown-up nurseries, whereas others will teach your children new skills or focus on sporting or technology activities.

Those with bigger groups and less equipment tend to be the most affordable, and it's worth investigating which clubs and camps your children's classmates will be attending so that you know they'll have fun, and you can set up lift-sharing too. Sharing childcare with other parents via play dates is also a great option for school holidays.

Lift-sharing, play dates and sleepovers

Some childcare settings are significantly less formal than others. Another for our informal category alongside family help is help from your wider support network. As your children grow older and cement their school friendships and activity schedules, their social lives will quickly get fuller than yours. Rather than becoming their chauffeur, diary organiser, personal assistant and caterer, it's time to get strategic. Can their busy social life free up some of your time so that you can create one of your own? Make sure that you get friendly with the parents of the other children in your child's social circles.

They will almost definitely want some time off too. If they play football, or swim or dance at the weekends, organise a rota of lift-sharing with one or more of the other parents so that you can take at least every other week off to do something for yourself. If they are always asking for a sleepover with their best mate and you're comfortable with your child also staying there, speak to their parent/s and see if they could take it in turns in consecutive holidays or weekends.

Slowly but surely, you will become more comfortable with saying 'yes' to offers of help from the people around you. Obviously, your children's safety is the key priority here, so make sure you know parents well before trusting them with the care of your children; trust your gut, and make sure your child is completely comfortable too. But if your child has grown up with the same group of school friends, the chances are some of their parents will be like an extended family by now, and you will have helped them out with school runs or lifts as many times as they have helped you. Timing sleepover requests for when you have a work trip, a date or you're on the brink of burnout isn't sneaky – it's just good sense.

My single-parent story

Ruth Talbot, solo mother of three, writer and founder of the campaign group Single Parent Rights

I separated from my husband when my first son was seven months old, and we were divorced not long later. It was a very bad relationship by the end, and he's not had much involvement since. A couple of years later I chose to have another child via donor conception. I've since had another son this way. I've been a single mum for almost nine years.

I think your path to single parenthood defines your early challenges in many ways. I became a single mum through trauma and that's hard to overcome when you're also parenting a little one solo. People expect separation and divorce to mean the end of a difficult relationship, but instead it just shifts. There's very little spoken about that, and it took me time to understand. The first couple of years were a complete head spin. I lurched from crisis to crisis with my ex, and ultimately had a breakdown; however, going on to have another two children solo, while of course challenging, has also been the best and most empowering thing I've done. It's the lack of a second person to share it all with that I find hardest, though, even after almost nine years of doing this. It's not even about wanting to share the heavy lifting (though that would be nice), I'm a dab hand at multitasking, and not much fazes me, but having no one to compare notes with when you're worried about the baby's breathing, or no one to smile in amazement with when your son takes his first steps, those are the really hard parts. It's also just about being an adult with no partner. Life can be hard: work, friendships, health scares, losing people, life is a tough journey at times, and having no one who is your person through that journey creates a gnawing loneliness that can be hard to shake, especially when you add trauma to the mix.

My proudest moment of being a single parent is, actually, becoming one. In the early days of first becoming a single mum that meant putting one foot in front of the other while my world was collapsing. And I did it. I kept my son healthy and happy. I kept my job. I kept my home. I did it all. Becoming a single mum all over again, not once, but twice, in very different circumstances has been amazing.

My household is chaotic and challenging, even on the good days, but there's not one second when I regret expanding my family this way. I'm so proud I took this path and so grateful every day to have my family of three and the freedom I have to do exactly what I want, when I want.

I'm also pretty chuffed that I've taken the kids travelling around the globe solo to Thailand, Kenya and across Europe. They might remember the house being cold and the Christmas stockings lacking in expensive gifts, but hopefully they will also remember some of the amazing things we've done together instead, and in the long run, it's those moments that will really count.

In those early days of parenting alone, I wish I'd known that it was the start of something new, not merely the end of something old. It turns out that plan B can be pretty wonderful too. I also wish I'd known that there was no need to feel ashamed about my marriage ending. It wasn't a failure, just a part of the ebb and flow of life. Perhaps unusually, I also wish I'd known just how hard it was going to be, that it doesn't always get easier with time and that learning to ask for support (which I'm still crap at) is the only way to get through, sometimes.

Ruth's advice

Keep going. In the early days it can be an explosion of emotions depending on how you got here. Whether that's a (misplaced) sense of shame, or the euphoria of hope that you might now be able to enjoy life. It's a rollercoaster and often just getting through is hard. In time you'll find your rhythm. And although we can't use positive thinking to overcome major trauma or serious hardship, to a certain extent life is what you make it. You can still do all the things you wanted to do; it's just that now you don't have to pick up someone else's socks too.

4

Let's Talk Money, Honey – Finances

'To be financially independent is to be self-sufficient. To be your own safety net. And that should be something single parents should be striving for with a tunnel vision attitude.'

Natalye-Marrie Boyce, financial freedom coach and founder of The Lone Parent

We need to talk about money.

If you've separated and become a single parent, the chances are that your household income just dropped by 50 per cent or more, and if you're having a baby on your own, life just got a whole lot more expensive. It might feel that things are about to get a little tricky on the money management front. We'd be lying if we said that you were wrong, but the good news is that you're not alone. Throughout this chapter we share advice from single-parenting money coach Natalye-Marrie Boyce, and we will be running you through all the things to think about when it comes to finances, from consolidating debts and smart saving, to ensuring all the bills are in your name. From the big picture to the details (like changing pass-words so that nobody else has access to your accounts), this chapter will give you an overview of how to get your finances looking significantly healthier.

Radical honesty

Step one: don't bury your head in the sand! Like many other chapters in this book, success in this area requires radical honesty, and a good deal of bravery. If money management has never been your forte, it can be tempting to look the other way rather than tackling shared bank accounts, mortgages, debts and credit ratings. But financial independence is absolutely imperative, not just for you, but for your children too. Until you have complete financial independence, you will not feel totally free, or in control of your own destiny, and you may struggle to feel completely safe too.

Financial independence won't look the same for everyone. For some, who were previously financially dependent on a partner, part of your financial security in the immediate future may be reliant on contributions from your co-parent or an ex-spouse. You may even need financial contributions from friends or family in the very short term, or rely on loans or credit. But making sensible choices and keeping borrowing to a minimum will get you to a position of sustainable financial independence as quickly as possible.

For many single parents, this will be the first time you've really thought about this side of life. Helen Thorn, author of *Get Divorced, Be Happy*, says: 'Taking control of finances is a really big thing. I had an ex who said "you don't need a pension, I'll always look after you" or "you don't need to worry about money, we have a joint account". I didn't really have my own bank account, you know, all those sort of things. So that was one of the biggest things. I never used to open my bank statements. And now I sit down, face them and budget to make sure I've got enough money.'

This is hard

The truth is, many economic systems are now structured on the basis of two earners per household. Life is getting more expensive, and in many cases wages aren't rising with costs. If you are finding it difficult to make your single-parent finances add up, you aren't alone. Natalye-Marrie says: 'Statistically, single parents have a hard time financially. In the UK, there are 1.8 million single families (source: Gingerbread) and half of them are living in poverty (source: the *Guardian*). Meanwhile, the US has the highest number of single parents in the world (the UK has the second highest), with a quarter of US children living in single-parent homes. Around 30 per cent of these single parents are living in poverty (source: the Annie Casey foundation).'

If you are struggling, it isn't your fault. Single parents are set up to fail (or at least to struggle) in many cases, and this is not a reflection on your capability as a single parent. If you need help, know that you are not alone. But putting a plan in place to guide yourself towards financial freedom is possible at any stage.

What really matters?

Getting a roof over your head and food on the table are your main short- to mid-term priorities, so financing those objectives should be at the top of your agenda. It might mean downgrading your accommodation, making more cost-effective choices at the supermarket, buying second-hand or switching up your mode of transport. But remembering that your children's main requirements are love, food and a happy home, rather than guest rooms and new cars, will steer you well when making these choices. This is not about getting rich quick, it is about learning to prioritise, budget and make responsible financial decisions that will stand you and your children in good stead for the future.

We are here to help you answer the important questions that every newly single parent needs to think about, and then get you started on how and where you can make savings and increase your bank balance. There is a lifetime of increased financial responsibility (but also freedom) ahead, and it's important that you take these first steps cautiously and with access to the right tools, rather than a 'put it all on black' gamble.

Financial control

First off, a note on a serious issue. In domestic abuse cases that involve financial control, going it alone can feel virtually impossible. Leaving might be essential, but it could feel impossible if you have little or no access to independent finances. If you are in an unhappy or even unsafe home, and you can't afford to leave, or you know someone in this situation, seeking professional help and support is essential. Search 'domestic abuse services near me' and speak to professionals that can provide you with information, support and options to get you safely away and on your way to freedom and independence. Once you have separated, an abusive ex might attempt to continue to use access to money to control you or your situation.

Seeking professional help and support in these cases is absolutely imperative, rather than going it alone. Breaking free from your abuser is always the best option for you and your child, no matter how much money they are trying to use to lure you back under their control. Refer to our advice from psychotherapist Charlotte Fox Weber on page 56 if you're co-parenting with an abuser.

Money is not happiness

Many of us know somebody who has wanted to leave an unhappy marriage (or we might even have been that person) but have stayed because they 'couldn't afford to leave'. To those people we say this: perhaps you cannot afford to stay.

It is true to some extent that most people 'cannot afford to leave', but they are failing to finish the sentence. They cannot afford to leave and maintain the exact same lifestyle. Financial adjustments will have to be made. Many would-be solo parents believe that they 'cannot afford to have a baby' but the truth is that they 'cannot afford to have a baby ... without making financial adjustments or sacrifices'. As with all things in life, it is about making difficult choices and thinking about what really makes us happy. Is it having plenty of disposable cash? Or is it living in a safe and happy home with limited financial or material resources but endless love, freedom and emotional independence? Money is not happiness. It is a means to survival.

Start viewing happiness as the most important currency, and you'll realise what you *really* can and can't afford to do.

Financial independence

Nothing, and we mean nothing, provides freedom like financial independence. Money, whether earned or unearned, is a ticket to an easier life (but not, as previously mentioned, a ticket to happiness). As a single parent, achieving financial independence should be the ultimate goal. When your child or children are in your care, being able to provide for them fully and without support means that you will have to answer to nobody, and you can focus on how you choose to provide for them and raise them. This doesn't mean that you may not need support, either from time to time or on an on-going basis, but if you can achieve this by independent means (such as via a social care system, formalised child support or private support) rather than relying on casual contributions, you will be able to build a secure foundation as a single parent that both you and your children can rely on.

However you are providing financial stability, your independence in this area comes from taking responsibility for your finances. This means getting your head around exactly where your money is coming from, and where it is going. There are endless things to keep on top of: there are costs for accommodation, childcare, bills, insurance payments, food, travel, clothing – the list goes on. There are savings to be made and there are extra streams of income you can find. Identifying them means educating yourself on exactly how your finances operate and seeking help if you need it to make improvements.

Security

Ultimately, financial independence is about security: both yours and your children's. Many single parents have never managed their own finances (at least not all elements of them) before. Some are even tempted to allow an ex-partner or third party to continue taking care of this side of things. But this is a big mistake. Imagine letting someone else be in charge of the keys to your home. Instead of knowing that you've locked the front door after leaving, you're just hoping someone else has done it. You're not checking that the hot water hasn't been left running, you're just hoping someone else has turned the taps off. You're hoping nothing drastic has happened or that things are slowly falling out of windows but you're never quite sure. This would not feel safe, or secure.

Treating your finances like this will not lead to financial security or stability. Avoiding looking at our finances will simply not work; we have to address them head on. There are several key considerations when you're safeguarding your financial security. Natalye-Marrie says: 'You need to think about building an emergency fund, clearing those high-interest debts such as the credit cards, overdrafts, store cards and payday loans.'

Consolidating debts into one low-interest loan that you have a strict timetable to pay off with one monthly payment is a great start. And once you've taken care of high-interest debts, starting a saving plan, however small, should be your goal. This will form the basis of your emergency fund.

Childcare costs

Once you've taken care of accommodation and food, there are some additional parenting expenses to consider. Natalye-Marrie says: 'Considerations will vary depending on the financial situation of the individual, but the common things to think about are: childcare costs, child maintenance and income after your maternity leave ends.'

In Chapter 3, we ran through the main types of childcare, so once you've thought about what would work for you, it's time to think about how to finance it. Natalye-Marrie says: 'We all know that childcare is extremely expensive, so firstly go to the gov.uk website [or your country's equivalent] and use the childcare calculator. It will work out what you're eligible for based on the number of hours you'll work and your income. Depending on your earnings you could be eligible for up to 30 hours of free childcare and tax-free childcare, with planned reforms expanding this free childcare entitlement to children as young as nine months in the coming years.

'Next, have a think about what kind of childcare you would like. Would you like your child to attend a nursery, have a childminder, stay with family, have a nanny or do a little with family and then spend a couple of days at a nursery? Nannies are generally more expensive, but you could do a nanny share to help bring down the costs.'

Child maintenance

As we have already said, if you can get yourself to a position where you don't rely on child maintenance, so much the better. But, of course, this will not be possible for everyone, especially in the short term. 'If you have a good co-parenting relationship with your ex, then I wouldn't even involve the government in your dealings,' says Natalye-Marrie. 'Both you and your ex should sit down and discuss what the child needs at this moment and decide how often payments will be made.'

Like all aspects of parenting, this will be subject to change. Natalye-Marrie says: 'I will stress that this conversation should not be a one-time thing. It should be ongoing. Babies grow up and become toddlers, then primary- and secondary-aged children, so their financial costs will definitely increase as they get older. This needs to be acknowledged during the first conversation so that both parties know what to expect.

Of course, not all co-parents will be agreeable. 'If your relationship with your ex is not agreeable, I would go straight to the Child Maintenance Service (CMS),' says Natalye-Marrie. She warns: 'However, do not expect too much. They can only work out accurate payments if the person is employed. If the person is self-employed, they will go on whatever that person tells them. For example, you know your ex makes around £100k a year, however because he/she is self-employed they can tell the CMS "Well, actually I run a business, but it's only breaking even and my take-home pay is around £1k a month. These are my bills and rent,' and so on. CMS will make a calculation based on that, and you may get nothing.

Your goal, ultimately, should be financial independence, that glorious utopia we keep banging on about. 'Whatever camp you are in, do not depend on your ex financially,' says Natalye-Marrie. 'Make it a goal that whatever your ex gives you is a bonus and not a necessity. Whether you have a great co-parenting relationship with them or not, having to rely on someone outside your control to help you with your bills is a big no.'

Lone parents

If you're coming into single parenthood from the birth of your child or as a lone parent, prepare to see how you feel and allow yourself to change your mind and career goals.

'We never know how we're going to feel about going back

to work until the baby arrives,' says Natalye-Marrie. 'When I had my daughter, I was still about the 9 to 5 lifestyle and its 40-plus-hour weeks, and after 11 months I sent her to nursery and went back to work full-time; however, when my son arrived, I knew the full-time work life was no longer for me and I wanted to be at home with my children and create an income that didn't drag me away from them for 40 hours every week. Whatever camp you fall in, if you don't have a financial plan, you'll need to create one. Think about what you would like to earn to be comfortable and how you would like to earn it. If you have to go back to work and work the same hours you did before you went on maternity leave, but you don't want to do it indefinitely, create a plan and execute it.'

Financial aid

As much as you want to make the numbers add up, sometimes they simply will not. As we already said, some systems simply do hot support single-parent families living on one standard wage, and however hard you work, sometimes it is simply not enough. Knowing what support is available to you, if this is the case for you, should be at the top of your to-do list. Universal credit, the NHS low-income scheme, council tax reduction and child benefits are all available in the UK, and being in receipt of many of these also qualifies your child for extra support in their education setting, such as free school meals or contribution towards extra-curricular activities. We spoke to several single parents who have utilised financial aid to make things work, you'll find two of their stories at the end of this chapter.

Budget

Create a plan, and execute it. You heard Natalye-Marrie! Have we convinced you to get those finances in order? Great, let's do it then. She says: 'Living below your means is important, and it won't be achievable until you put a budget in place. Unfortunately, people want to bypass budgeting, which is probably one of the main causes of them running out of money before their next pay hits their account. Most people's financial problems are due to spending, not income.'

This is a key point, and hails back to the point we made earlier. In many cases, it isn't that you haven't got enough money, it's that you haven't got enough money to do everything you would like to do. Your income might not be the issue, but rather, what you're spending that income on. The only way to find out is to make a thorough budget.

How do we make this easy? Is there a secret? A hack? 'Ha! Sadly there is no secret,' says Natalye-Marrie. 'Budgeting is boring, hence why people do not want to do it. It's not sexy, juicy or exciting, but implementing a budget consistently over time will yield good results. You don't need any fancy apps – pen and paper is just fine.'

So grab your pen and paper and let's do this.

Whys and hows

'The way to stick to a budget is to firstly ensure that you know your goals and the reason behind your goals (your "whys"),' says Natalye-Marrie. 'For example, I wanted to run a business because I wanted to make money (this is the "goal") without compromising my time with my children, and I was tired of having to work with colleagues who lacked emotional intelligence, creating a toxic working culture (this is the "why").

'Once you've written down your "goals" and your "whys", you then need to understand your spending habits and how that has affected you. You do this by looking over the last three months of bank statements. Now you can create your budget.'

Your budget should include all money in (earnings, interest, child maintenance, benefits or tax credits) and all outgoings. Remember that the goal here is not to balance the books per se, but to ensure that your outgoings are lower than your incomings. It is by creating this surplus that you will find true financial freedom. You can write this using pen and paper, create an Excel spreadsheet (this is a good option, because it is easy to update digitally and share if you need to, making comparisons over time and auto-calculating figures), or make use of a budgeting app. Many bank accounts and apps now have budgeting tools or saving helpers built in, so once you have gone through all your finances you may find it easier to make use of these.

If you haven't done so already, pause now and make your budget.

No really, don't keep reading until you've done it.

'Once you've created your budget, you'll need to track your spending,' says Natalye-Marrie. 'I always recommend doing this by hand using pen and paper. This gives you accountability in real time and shows you that the problem is not your income but your spending habits.'

Emotional spending

Spending can be seriously addictive, and a level of emotional work to break or adjust habits may be needed here.

Addressing this sooner rather than later will lead to a greater chance of financial success. Natalye-Marrie's advice for this is as follows: 'Track your emotions. Your emotions control your spending. And a great way to track your emotions is to journal them.

'Whenever you feel like spending (impulse buying) that is not planned (that is, in your budget) instead of picking up your debit or credit card, pick up a pen and notebook and write down what's coming up for you. Use prompts such as "What am I feeling right now? Where is this coming from? What is it that I really need?" Self-awareness and emotional intelligence is so important and is connected to our money.'

Realising the tie between what we're spending, and how it is making us feel (long and short term) can help to break some unhealthy habits when it comes to managing our finances.

Helen Thorn put this into action to change her spending habits: 'Look at all your incidental spending, but also look at what that spending does to you emotionally,' she says. 'I remember buying a new outfit because I was feeling really sad. So why was I spending that money and for what gain? That's a really good thing to think about.'

Making cuts

Once you've made your budget and addressed what is motivating your spending, you might need to make some additional cuts. Doing things in this order is important, says Natalye-Marrie. 'Get your mindset right before you start cutting back, because otherwise you'll struggle and suffer.'

It is also important to realise that we are not defined by our bank balance, just as we are not defined by our single-parent status. 'Remember that your reduced income is temporary.

This isn't your forever, so do not define yourself with that. It's just a life circumstance and life circumstances are not who we are, nor do they last for ever.'

You won't be able to wipe out essential spending, but you might be able to make small reductions by doing your research and investing your time in getting clued up. 'Look at your essential spend and see where you can maybe get the same but for cheaper, such as changing mobile phone providers, changing your car and home insurance providers, and so on.'

Again, Helen Thorn put this into action in her early single-parent days. 'Even just going on those comparison websites, I think I saved something crazy, like 1,000 quid a year just from doing a few little switches. And it took a couple of hours.'

There are other ways you can reduce spending. Think about buying school uniforms second-hand, and utilise hand-me-downs and charity shops for your clothes, and the kids'. Not only will this save you money, but it's better for the planet too. Rental sites are ways to access little luxuries for shorter periods of time, and you can even increase your income by renting any luxe or designer clothes in your wardrobe too.

Once you have streamlined your essentials as much as possible, it is time to think about sacrifices. 'Next, go to your wants and start eliminating what you can live without temporarily and then look at what you can reduce,' says Natalye-Marrie. 'For example, at the beginning of my financial journey, I got rid of my TV. At the time it was temporary, but it changed into permanent because I saw how productive I was when I removed distraction. Beauty treatments are a want but I will not give them up, so I decided to go to my local college where they had a beauty salon for their beauty students to practise. I would go there to get some of my beauty treatments for a third of what I would have been paying if I went to a fully qualified salon.'

Being flexible on a shoestring is also possible, so overpaying on your mortgage or saving a little on quiet months is a possibility, as is increasing your bank balance by being creative with your assets. Ruth Talbot, founder of the Single Parent Rights campaign, says: 'Don't spend where you don't need to, so that you can afford some of the niceties. Of course, this only works if you're above the breadline, which in today's climate is becoming harder and harder. But I rarely buy the kids' clothes, instead I get hand-me-downs and free stuff from local groups. It's the same for furniture. With food, I always buy the cheapest possible and the heating has barely been on since 2021. As a homeowner with a mortgage, if there's any money in the account come payday, I put it onto the mortgage as an overpayment. You can usually overpay by 10 per cent annually without a penalty, though you should check this with your lender. I'm of the "every little counts" mentality and I've also become a dab hand at making money in other ways. I have rented my spare room on Airbnb and my driveway through Just Park and my holidays are usually funded through renting my entire home out on Airbnb.'

Invest in yourself

If you can afford it, don't rule out spending on yourself completely. If you can set a little aside in your budget for a treat or a self-care experience each month, you should. Socialising is incredibly important, but it might feel that you have to cut back here too, especially if your non-single-parent friends have a penchant for expensive meals out or cocktails on the town. It is about making adjustments in this area as well, rather than ruling out spending altogether. Helen Thorn says: 'In the beginning it was all about delivery pizzas, but if I just went to a budget supermarket and got a few frozen pizzas, I'd save about £7,000 a year. And also having nights in with friends, especially if you can't get childcare, rather than going out. There's nothing wrong with saying, "Look, you bring the pudding, I'll make lasagne," add a couple of five-quid bottles of wine, it's just as fun as going out and getting drunk in the pub.'

And if Helen is hosting, we couldn't agree more.

Pension

For much of single parenthood you are living in the moment and simply putting one foot in front of the other. You can feel as if life is only about rolling with the punches and seeing what it throws at you next. This is fine to some extent, but planning for the future is important. Planning for your retirement is something you might also want to start thinking about once your day-to-day spending is in order. This is thinking about things such as company benefits – for example, enhanced pension contributions – or researching private pensions or longer-term investments if you are self-employed. The state pension age is ever increasing and not intended to be a sole income source, so having a financial plan for retirement is advisable. Remember that your financial security is also that of your children.

One thing at a time

Before we leave you, just one final piece of advice on overcoming the financial hurdles that come your way during single parenthood. 'Deal with financial issues one at a time,' says financial-freedom coach Natalye-Marrie. 'Trying to do them all simultaneously will be overwhelming, then it will cause paralysis and you'll feel unmotivated and won't believe that you can achieve your financial goals.'

One step at a time – this time next year we'll be millionaires!

Financial aid: real stories

We reached out to members of the Frolo single-parent community and asked for stories about accessing financial aid. Two single parents share their stories here.

Solo dad George,* 56

I became a solo dad due to safeguarding issues after my divorce in 2017. My son and I have grown very close and are like best friends as well as father and son. Coping financially was a big challenge. I had already requested term-time working hours to be able to care for my son's needs while still being able to work, but this was to prove extremely difficult because my company refused. For two years I battled, and I was eventually granted my original request: to be able to work term time with equated pay spread over each month. This was a massive victory for myself and my son.

I have had financial aid, via Universal Credit (UC), due to my income being low and the amount of time needed to care for my son. I was informed after speaking with Citizens Advice that I could claim UC and carer's allowance, which I did to help top up my wages each month. I budgeted my income to cover household bills, food and fuel. It's been very difficult, and I've even had to use the food bank to make ends meet when I was off work ill.

I consider myself very fortunate, and even though I struggle on my own, I've always tried to help others and remain positive. Often things happen that are out of your hands, no matter how hard you try to fix things. Moving on from the past can, and will, be challenging at times for some, but coming to terms with this will help you to move forward. Set yourself some new goals, and take care of yourself as well as your children. I spend 100 per cent of my time with my son or on my own when he's at school or I'm at work. Frolo is my new family. The community understands what you've been through; they offer helpful advice, support you when you're feeling low and make you laugh to brighten your day.

Solo mother Susan,* 33

My marriage was unhealthy, and I finally saw the true reality of who I was living with a long time after I should have. My friends and family had known for some time, but I finally saw the mental abuse for what it was; the penny dropped and I knew I had to keep my children safe. It had been brewing for some time, but I finally felt brave enough to gather some things and leave.

I went from a family home with two incomes, to moving back to my parents with a minimal income and increasing childcare costs. As a family, we'd lived quite comfortably, and I'd shopped for groceries without concern and thought nothing of getting my hair and nails done. These little luxuries I'd once afforded myself are now gone, because I can't justify the expense when I'd rather spend the money on something that benefits the children too.

When I left, I was frightened and anxious. I knew I couldn't replicate the missing income, and I worried about how I'd keep us moving, how I'd pay the credit cards that were conveniently all in my name, how I'd pick myself up and get back on my feet. I knew I wanted to buy a home for my children – I don't want to pay someone else's mortgage and be at the mercy of a landlord. I recognise that I'm in a fortunate position where I can live with my parents and keep saving, but even this feels like a very long process. I feel a long way from my end goal. I had to shrug off the negative feelings about accepting state help and find out how to help my children and I get on.

I had to list all my monthly outgoings, I needed to see them in black and white – needed to truly understand what the picture looked like. I have a spreadsheet now, which records everything, including the savings I make and the remaining debts. I had to, and still have to, see it all in front of me. Although I knew I would never have judgement from my family, I felt that I needed to keep some level of independence, and I didn't want to share the complete picture. I don't talk to them about my financial situation.

I do receive state help – and I feel better now about admitting that, but it's taken some time. I felt embarrassed when I first used the 'turn2us' calculator to see what I was entitled to. I felt like my situation wasn't 'desperate' enough, and I didn't want to be in the position where I had to accept help – but I quickly realised that no one wants to be in that position. Everyone values independence. It is just that at this point, right now, there isn't another way. My children are too young for me to work full-time, though I desperately miss that. But this time comes once, they'll only be this little once – and while there is help to make things a bit easier, I should take it. I can return to full-time work when they're older and in school full-time.

My financial situation is constantly on my mind. I don't ever feel at ease and I feel awful for buying anything that doesn't constitute a necessity. I think I'm too hard on myself, but now that I'm the only one my children are relying on, I feel like I have to have 'it all together'. Some days my end goal, our home, feels impossible. But I know I need to be patient, I need to keep trudging and making the smallest savings where I can because it all adds up. Eventually, I'll have the keys to my own front door and I'll be so proud when I do. It'll all be on me!

My plan is to be able to buy them a home and reach a point where I feel stable and less worried month to month. I want to not have that stress in my head so that I can focus on being the absolute best mummy for them. But I know that earning more means you spend more, so actually everyone worries to some degree.

My advice for single parents in my situation is that the embarrassment is only in your head, everyone else is too busy dealing with their stories, and there is no need to fear judgement. The support is needed, it's there to help in these situations, and you won't need it for ever. But it'll help get you to a stronger position and to buy time to get yourself together in the way you wish to. Seek help from different government calculators, Citizens Advice, and other agencies to guide you. Work to minimise the costs you can control, but don't beat yourself up for the 'luxury' of a coffee-shop coffee once in a blue moon – sometimes you need these little things to keep you moving.

*names have been changed

5

Working 9 to 5 – and All Things to Do with Work

'Single parents are all too often faced with little choice but to take low-paid, part-time work which is below their skill set because they do not have access to affordable, flexible childcare, trapping single parents and their children in poverty.'

Gingerbread charity spokesperson

The job of parenting doesn't change when you go from a parenting team to a single parent. But your working hours and job responsibilities do.

We've covered in this book how to look after our money, but now: how to make it? The stereotype of the over-extended single parent working multiple jobs has long existed, and for good reason, but with the rise of flexible working and a growing number of remote opportunities, it doesn't necessarily have to be that way. As with all elements of single-parent life, there may need to be adjustments in this area. What worked for you pre-single-parent life may not be an option any more. Your priorities have likely changed, and your work life will need to too.

The fact is, all parents have to make adjustments if they

have parental responsibility, and this is even more evident for single and solo parents. We aren't here to tell you how to get rich quick (actually, if anyone does know how, please share), and we don't have the secrets to achieving the perfect work–life balance (again, answers on a postcard), but we have got some things for you to think about, and some lessons we've learnt along the way. The truth is that making work, well, work, will look completely different for every one of you, and different industries, roles and set-ups all require different adjustments and advice, but we've tried to cover some of the common threads that all single parents need to think about when it comes to maintaining a career alongside parenting.

Parenting *is* work

First things first, let's clear something up. Parenting is work. It is unpaid work, yes, but it is one of the most important jobs on the planet. Imagine for a second that you didn't have kids. You have a full-time job, and then you get offered a new, better and more exciting full-time job. But instead of resigning the first one, you decide to do both at once. Everyone would think you were mad. You now have two full-time jobs to do, but you have no more hours in the day.

Becoming a parent is like this, apart from the fact that the second job isn't 40 hours a week: it's 168. And if you're a solo parent, you don't even have the option of a job share. Prioritising your parenting over your work is not only understandable, but it is also admirable. If there are periods when you are unable to work full-time, unable to focus on furthering your career or even unable to work at all, due to your single-parenting commitments, it does not mean that you are failing as a single parent. It is close to impossible to survive economically, let alone thrive, as a single head of a household.

This is not the failing of single parents. This is a failing of the systems we exist within. It is a failing of the childcare system, lack of legal protection of working parents, lack of flexible working options and sub-par wages. If you are unable to support your children with your salary on your own and are forced to seek help, whether from the state or from a co-parent or family, you are not a failure. Sometimes not working is the only viable option, even if only for a short period, or until your children start school and you have regular hours within which to work. Once again, this is *not* a failure. The following advice is around how to make your career work better for you as a single parent. It won't be useful for everyone, because not everyone has the privilege of access to flexible working, freelance work, salary negotiations, hybrid work or working from home. The reality is that parents are being forced out of the workplace around the world for financial and logistical reasons. If you are at a point where you have to hit pause on your career, or at least on your career progression, just know that you will be able to hit unpause in time. And just as single parenting opens you up to a whole new world and life that you never knew you were aiming towards, it may be the opportunity you were waiting for to tear up your career plan and build a new and more exciting one too.

Know your rights

Working Families, the UK's national charity for working parents and carers (workingfamilies.org.uk), has put together a guide for us on the main rights that working single parents should be aware of.

Parental leave

If you have been an employee for more than one year, you can take unpaid parental leave to look after your child/children. You can take up to four weeks of parental leave per child per year (up to 18 weeks total). This is the legal minimum; it may be that your contract entitles you to more. You need to give 21 days notice to take this leave. Your employer cannot refuse your request, but they can postpone your leave if business would be particularly affected. If your employer wants to postpone your request, they must let you know within seven days of your request and they cannot change the length of leave requested. Parental leave usually needs to be taken in blocks of one week; however, if your child gets Disability Living Allowance (DLA), you can take leave in blocks of one day. Parental leave is usually unpaid unless that's a perk in your contract/employer's policy.

Time off for dependants

You have the right to take emergency time off for dependants. This time off is limited to use in unforeseen situations; for example, if your child is taken ill and you have to pick them up from school at short notice. It cannot be used as leave to cover periods where you know you will regularly not have childcare. Your employer cannot lawfully sack you for exercising your right to take time off for dependants, as long as the time taken was reasonable and necessary. What is reasonable depends on your personal circumstances. There is no fixed rule about what is reasonable, but bear in mind that your employer will expect you to use the time off for dependants to arrange care provision so that you can return to work. If you regularly take time off for dependants for foreseeable situations with childcare, this is likely to be seen as an unreasonable exercise of the right. Time off for dependants is usually unpaid, unless that's a perk in your contract/employer's policy or practice, and usually lasts for only a few days. If you need longer, your employer may ask you to take it as another type of leave, such as annual leave.

Discrimination at work

Along with your workplace rights, it is important to know what discrimination you are legally protected from in the workplace. Working Families say: 'Being a parent or carer is not a protected characteristic. However, parents and carers who experience unfair treatment at work due to their childcare or caring responsibilities may be covered under other protected characteristics, most likely: Sex; Pregnancy and Maternity; Disability.' They have laid these out for us here:

Direct sex discrimination

Direct sex discrimination can occur when a parent or carer is treated less favourably on the basis of their gender; for example, if an employer refuses to allow a father to work flexibly around his childcare responsibilities, but allows female colleagues to do so, because of sex (that is, because the employer believes men shouldn't have caring responsibilities), this would be an example of direct sex discrimination.

Indirect sex discrimination

Indirect sex discrimination can occur when an employer has a policy or practice that applies to everyone, but disadvantages women, and the policy or practice cannot be justified by the employer. Because women tend to have more childcare responsibilities than men, a policy or practice that disadvantages women because of their childcare responsibilities can amount to indirect sex discrimination. This is called childcare disparity, as it is evidenced women have more caring responsibilities than men. This argument can apply to employers who refuse a flexible working request, or a mother's request to work part-time, or require working patterns that are difficult to make work around childcare responsibilities. There does not need to be a formal policy in place for an employee to challenge an employer policy or practice on the basis of indirect sex discrimination. A one-off or discretionary management decision can be challenged as discriminatory.

Men cannot claim indirect sex discrimination for flexible working as the 'childcare disparity' only applies to women, but men might have a claim for direct sex discrimination if, for example, an employer lets women work flexibly but not men.

Harassment (on the basis of sex) – not the same as sexual harassment

Harassment could also occur on the basis of sex where an employer engages in unwanted conduct based on stereotypes of gender and parenting roles; for example, if an employer makes unwanted comments based on assumptions about a woman in connection to pregnancy, maternity or childcare.

Pregnancy and maternity discrimination

Pregnancy and maternity discrimination occurs when a woman is treated unfavourably because of her pregnancy, pregnancy-related illness, or intention to take maternity leave. Examples of pregnancy and maternity-related discrimination include dismissal, removal of responsibilities or seniority, a failure to offer a pay rise when you would have had one if you had been in work, or the refusal to promote or offer training because you have been on maternity leave. In order for it to be considered maternity or pregnancy discrimination, the unfavourable treatment must occur during what is called the 'protected period', which runs from when you become pregnant to the end of maternity leave. Unfavourable treatment because of pregnancy or maternity that happens outside of this period may amount to sex discrimination.

Associative disability discrimination

This can occur where a parent of a person with a disability is treated less favourably than others. Both direct discrimination and indirect discrimination can occur (although indirect associative disability discrimination is still a new territory and has not really been pushed high enough in the employment tribunals to get a precedent). The disability must have lasted longer, or is likely to last longer, than 12 months and affects day-to-day activities.

Part-time workers

Part-time workers are protected against being treated less favourably than full-time workers under the part-time workers regulations.

Financial support

Single parents should also be assured that financial support and help with childcare costs is available. Don't assume that you're not entitled to anything – it's worth using a benefits calculator to see what support might be available.

NOTE These rights are correct at the time of going to print, but may be subject to change and differ from country to country. Visit workingfamilies.org.uk for more help and advice, and visit the Resources section at the end of this book for more helpful websites and services, in other countries.

Stand your ground

Ruth Talbot (founder of the campaign group Single Parent Rights) says the following in relation to discrimination in the workplace: 'As single parents, we are often treated unfairly. Unfortunately, we don't have protection from direct discrimination in the UK Equality Act, which is why I've set up the campaign group Single Parent Rights to push for us to be given legal protection from discrimination; however, in the meantime, if you're a single mum and you face discrimination at work, this might count as indirect sex discrimination, as the majority of single parents are women. I would always advise people to be a member of a union, as they will support you, including legal representation, where appropriate. Even if your employer doesn't formally recognise a union, you can still join one. If you're not a union member and you face discrimination, you can try legal helplines for support. Keep records of everything that's happened, and when, and be prepared to fight your corner.'

Working Families have produced a helpful guide for if you do feel that you are facing discrimination in the workplace as a single parent:

1 **Try to resolve the issue** Speak to your employer in the first instance and try to resolve things informally. Try to keep communications friendly if you can. It can sometimes be more effective if you focus on solutions and the way forward, rather than the things you are unhappy about. Often, employers can become defensive if accused of discrimination, but you can say if you think you are being treated unfairly because of a protected characteristic.

2 **Raise a grievance** If the discussions with your employer don't resolve the issue, or you think your employer has treated you very unfairly and the relationship is breaking down, you can consider raising a grievance. Raising a grievance is important if you think you might later raise a claim in the employment tribunal because failure to follow internal resolution methods can disadvantage your claim. It is advisable to try to resolve things amicably, as formal processes can damage your relationship with your employer. Your employer should not ignore your grievance, fail to hear it within a reasonable time or reject it out of hand (as doing so could amount to a breach of your employment contract); however, your employer is not obliged to uphold your complaint.

3 **Make a claim in the employment tribunal** If the above steps do not resolve the matter, you could bring a claim in the employment tribunal. Proving discrimination claims can be difficult, as the discrimination is rarely made explicit. The tribunal will follow a two-stage 'burden of proof' test. You must contact ACAS to start early conciliation within three months less a day of the act of discrimination. Tribunal claims can be stressful and long, and there is no guarantee of success, so this step should be considered cautiously. It is often best to try to resolve the issue with your employer. If you are considering bringing a claim, you should get legal advice.

Precious time

Single parenting is the fastest route to learning the value of your own time. From the moment your baby is born, time takes on a new meaning: time between feeds, time between naps, time between nappy changes. Routines are endlessly discussed (and executed with varying levels of success). Minutes and hours of sleep are lost and found. The precious daytime naps become hives of productivity; you learn to do entire days of work in an hour or two of peace. Every (hands-on) parent receives this (largely unwelcome) time-management training, and it is absolutely vital for single parents to apply it to their working lives. Those snatches of downtime as baby sleeps help you to really value your 'free' time. Putting a monetary value on this time is how to make your work work for you. Figuring out how much you need to earn, and how many hours you have to earn it in, are the first steps in making work work for you as a single parent.

Working 9 to 5

Firstly, we don't know about you, but forget 9 to 5, it feels like the average working day has crept closer to 9 to 6. And with the average school day running from 9 to 3, something's got to give when it comes to working single parents. Being in an office from 9am until 6pm five days a week just isn't realistic for most working parents, especially if you're on your own. Likewise, shift work or working evenings or weekends is tricky if childcare or educational settings hold set day-time hours.

Your options are to find childcare to fit your working hours, or working hours to fit your childcare, and this decision is likely going to come down to finances. If you have access to free or affordable childcare within certain hours, it is likely going to be the better option to find work that fits this rather than the other way around. Figuring out your ideal working hours is a good start if you are going to need to make changes now that you're a single parent.

WFH

Working from home used to be incredibly rare pre-pandemic, but since almost every office-based job went fully remote in 2020 when lockdowns hit, homeworking has become a permanent fixture for many. If you have the option to find work in a field that gives you the option for home working, your capacity to earn as a single parent will increase enormously. Being a single parent means being housebound for large chunks of time, when you're at home with your kids. If you can do your job from home, you might be able to do it when the children are in the house sometimes too. You may even be able to catch up in the evenings when they're in bed, allowing you freedom in the day to be there for the children for school runs or mealtimes. This means that you will have the capacity to earn without the need for childcare. You might be able to work evenings or weekends to increase your available working hours, thus increasing your capacity to earn. Obviously, this simply doesn't work for many careers that involve customer or public-facing jobs, but if you would be open to retraining or side-stepping, or you can find a way to make changes to your work situation that would allow for home working, life might become just that little bit easier.

Flexible working

At the time of writing, in the UK, 'All employees have the legal right to request flexible working – not just parents and carers'; however, your employer's only responsibility is to deal with your request in a 'reasonable manner'. Reasonable is one of the most subjective words in the English language, so the results of these requests are going to be quite varied; however, if you can obtain access to flexible working, you might just be able to juggle your career with your most important job: as a parent.

Working out the available working hours you have, as mentioned above, allows you to envision how your ideal working week would look to you. Even if you don't have a job that allows for home working, you may be able to make changes to your schedule that will fit these hours. Requesting flexible working hours will mean that you work hours outside your usual contracted hours, or you have a working week that involves a mixture of short and long days to ease the strain on your childcare needs. If you've been in the same job for some time and you have a good relationship with your employer or line manager, you might be surprised at how willing they are to accommodate a change to your working schedule.

One single mother we spoke to, who is a nurse with 50 per cent custody of her children, has completely changed her shift pattern since separating from her husband, giving her one week of long 12-hour shifts and one much lighter week when she has the kids with her. By shifting from a weekly working week to a fortnightly one, she found a new working schedule that worked for her, without having to drop hours or pick up additional childcare costs. Her employer supported her in this, as well as supporting further studies to progress her career.

Alternatively, if your job allows for home working, negotiating a working week that has more WFH days and adjusted hours to allow for school runs or nursery pick-ups will mean you don't have to make massive changes to your job to fit your new single-parenting responsibilities.

The non-flexible bit

What do we need to know about flexible working requests? Working Families lays out the process for applying for flexible working, if you are a permanent employee. (Again, it's worth noting that this is a hot topic in employment law, so these rules are subject to change – hopefully in the stretchier, more flexible direction.)

'Any employee with 26 weeks service can make a statutory flexible working request,' say Working Families. 'Flexible working means changing the way you work and can include working less hours, working compressed hours, working from home, changing your start and finish times, or entering into a job share.

'Think about what you want, and where you can compromise. Try to see things from your employer's perspective. Our advice pages have lots of information on tips when making a flexible working request. You should state in your request if you are making the request due to childcare or in relation to the Equality Act (e.g. disability) if you are asking for flexible working to care for a child or disabled person. Your employer should give proper consideration to your request. You should also include details about the impact on family life if it is turned down.

'You can only make one statutory flexible working request in any 12-month period. If you have already made a statutory flexible working request within the last 12 months, you can still make an informal flexible working request. If your employer has refused your flexible working request, you may be able to challenge their decision in an employment tribunal if your employer breached the statutory procedure or if the refusal amounts to unlawful discrimination. If your request is refused, you should firstly appeal the decision.'

Family-friendly employers

Of course, there is a chance that your boss won't respond positively to requests to adjust your hours or introduce more remote working to fit your schedule. Or you might be looking for a new job after a period out of work now that your situation has changed. Or perhaps you're looking for a new stream of income and thinking about taking a part-time job. Either way, working for a company and/or a manager that is family friendly is vital to avoid adding extra stresses to your (already quite challenging) single-parent life.

Charities such as Working Families produce lists of the

best employers for working families, so it's worth scouring the news for companies doing things the right way. Speak to your friends about their jobs and see how they achieve a work–life balance, and look into vacancies that align with their positive advice. Ask for recommendations and referrals from peers and colleagues to employers that you know to be family friendly. You can check their policies on annual leave, sick days, flexible working, remote working, maternity and paternity policy and family-focused benefits. Perhaps they offer fully comprehensive health insurance that will cover you and your children. Maybe they have a generous pension package that will make you feel more secure as a single head of a family.

Whenever you go to a job interview, remember that as well as them interviewing you, you are interviewing them. Don't try to hide your circumstances, be clear about your needs and make sure that they will be sensitive to them. It's only going to lead to more stress in the long run if you play the role of someone who is solely focused on their career in an interview, because at least some of the time you are now going to be very heavily focused on your children, too, and hold sole responsibility for their care.

Be your own boss

Since you're currently on a bit of a roll when it comes to going solo, how about making the break away in your career too and becoming self-employed? It definitely won't work for every career, but for many jobs, the option for freelancing, consultancy work or becoming a sole trader is a very appealing possibility for single parents. Give some thought to how your job could lend itself to freelance work, and start exploring a plan to make it work. As a writer, Rebecca was able to add to her income with freelance journalism, copy-writing and editing, all of which would be completed at home to her own schedule as extra income alongside a staff magazine job at an independent magazine that allowed her to work flexibly and largely from home. Meanwhile, Zoë launched her own business, Frolo, which, while being an incredibly challenging ask of a newly single parent, involves home working and answering to herself rather than the demands of another. Many careers lend themselves to freelance, agency or consultancy work; reaching out to peers, forums or scouring LinkedIn might lend you some inspiration. The supportive single-parenting community might be just the place to find support or inspiration, so get on to Zoë's Frolo app and see if any of your new crew might be able to help you.

If you're fully self-employed and in receipt of financial support, you will need to make sure that you have a consistent stream of income to make the numbers add up. Working Families say: 'If you're on Universal Credit, it might be worked out on what you're expected to earn, rather than what you actually earn from self-employment. This means if your self-employed work fluctuates, you could have very little income some months as your Universal Credit might not increase to make up for low self-employed earnings in a month.'

Diversify your income

Speaking of freelancing, consultancy work and gig work, if you need to increase your earnings due to a change in circumstances (such as suddenly having to cover all the bills that you used to share, alone), diversifying your income is a great way to start. Not only does taking on a different kind of work in addition to your main job give you extra earning power, but it can also help to ease the pressure on one income stream, thus reducing your day-to-day work stress.

The additional work you do doesn't have to be related to your day-to-day job, either. At-home proof-reading, marking, starting an eBay or DePop shop, renting your clothes, a bar job, flyering, reception work that allows you time to complete other work at your desk ... think about what would fit into your life, and give it a go. This could also be a chance to aim towards your dream job, or start the business of your dreams from home. Start small and dip your toe in, whether it's with a few hours a week of consultancy work that you can do alongside your main job and scale up, or starting an Etsy shop to sell your art that you can run in your free time as a hobby. Gradually, you may be able to scale back on your 9 to 5 job and scale up the business that makes you really happy. Ruth Talbot told us: 'It will differ depending on your sector and role, but I've found part-time working suits me best. This is mainly because the finances don't add up to work full-time and pay for the necessary childcare. You have to be strict about sticking to your contracted hours though, as it's easy to get sucked in on your days "off". In addition, I am also trying to develop a portfolio career to help financially. So, while I have childcare to cover my office-based part-time work, I am also building my profile so that I can pick up the odd bit of work once the kids are asleep. It's tiring, but it's a great way to trial other careers without risking it all on quitting, as job security is so crucial as a single parent with no financial support. Of course, it doesn't work for all sectors, but if you can do it, it's a nice way to balance the security of a contracted role with the flexibility of freelance work.'

Tough conversations

Making many of these changes will involve having tough conversations. The first one you need to have is with yourself. How much money do you need to earn? How many hours do you have to earn it in? Do you want to be able to do school runs every day? Do you want to be able to take leave in school holidays or over nursery breaks? Can you work from home? Answering some of these basic questions will give you an idea of how much needs to change (if anything) in your work life to fit your new single-parenting set-up. The next tough conversation that you'll need to have is with your employer to facilitate the changes that you need to make work work for you. One tactic that works well for this is to remember the truth that all parents know but few choose to acknowledge: we all work for another boss now – the children. They call the shots, we answer to them, as much as we're the parents, we will all do just about anything to make them happy. When we are negotiating for a better set-up at work it can sometimes help to remember that we're doing so on behalf of our children, to be able to give them the best life possible and the happiest, most fulfilled parent possible. When the tough conversation you're about to have with your boss arises, or the one you might need to have in a year's time when your child's needs change, remember that as well as advocating for yourself, you are advocating for your kids. Nobody gets results like a parent pushing for better for their children.

My single-parent story

Linton Wadsworth, widower, solo father of three

I unfortunately lost my wife and partner-in-all of ten years to cervical cancer. She was diagnosed with stage-four cancer, and although she had promising initial reactions to chemotherapy and radiotherapy, things progressed aggressively. I have been a single parent for three years, but the sole carer of my children for approximately four years, as my wife was bedridden, either at home or at a hospice, for her last year.

Outside of managing the children through the grief of losing their mother, the toughest challenge was managing the logistics of how the children could continue with all their extracurricular activities now that there was no longer a second pair of hands to manage when clubs conflicted.

Since being a single parent, I have become much closer to the children than I was before. Previously, I focused heavily on my career, believing that my success at work was enabling my children to have access to more experiences at the expense of time with me. As a single dad, I have managed to readjust my work–life balance so that although I may not be progressing as much as I would have liked to in a professional sense, I have been able to ensure that I am present for all of my children's key events at school or their clubs.

I wish I'd known that modern workplaces seem to be much more understanding of the pressures of single parenthood than I realised. Being a child of a single parent myself in the 1990s I was aware of the challenges my mum had with managing a job and raising me; however, when I finally approached my workplace with a proposition on how I would like to work, they were much more amenable to the changes I needed than I had expected. If I had known this sooner, I wouldn't have suffered so much anxiety and stress in the early days of being a carer for my wife, and a widower.

Linton's advice

It's easy to focus on putting your children first, and think that by doing so, no matter what, you are doing right by them. It took me a long time to realise (with lots of heavy coaxing from other single parents) that this cannot be your only source of energy to manage single parenthood. Instead, rediscovering my own identity, rather than solely being a dad, actually gave me much more energy to be around the kids. I put more effort into my social life and dating so that my life didn't just become the cycle of waking up, taking the kids to school, going to work, picking up the kids, eat, sleep, rinse and repeat. Instead of being 'selfish', as was my original perception, it actually reintroduced more joy to the day, which helped when being a single parent became tough.

6

Is That Even Legal? –
Legal Considerations

'"Going legal" if your relationship breaks down can be
a knee-jerk reaction that costs huge amounts of cash and
ends the prospect of a working co-parenting relationship.
Instead, take a pause and a step back.'

Kate Daly, co-founder of Amicable, the couples' online
divorce service, and host of The Divorce Podcast

Single parents often focus on day-to-day survival in the early
days of their journey, and although that is understandable,
the legal matters need to be addressed sooner rather than
later too. You are now solely responsible, whether full- or
part-time, for the life of one or more children, and you must
consider what will happen to them if anything should change
in their personal circumstances. Every single parent should
ideally have access to a lawyer or at least know where to find
legal help should they need it. What are the legal considerations for co-parents? What things should you consider as
an adoptive solo parent? Do you know how to access legal
support if your workplace seems to be unwilling to support
your changing needs as a single parent?

For many, this will be the first time of thinking about

anything remotely legal, so the temptation to avoid looking at it in the eye and to swiftly change the subject whenever your thoughts turn to legal matters, will be strong. Doing this would be a mistake. Simply leaving the legal side of things to a professional (or your child's other parent) would be equally remiss, as you may end up with a situation that doesn't work for you, or you could be paying out on expensive legal fees unnecessarily.

Common ground

There are certain common legal issues that all single parents, no matter their circumstances, need to be aware of, and to take care of. There is a little crossover between legal and financial matters and housing, but it's important that you take care of all joint affairs from a legal perspective. A spokesperson from UK single-parent charity Gingerbread says: 'If you have become a single parent through separation, make sure you contact your bank if you have a joint account or share a credit card with your ex-partner to let them know about your change in circumstance.' Once you have taken care of joint finances, getting your housing circumstances cemented is the next step. This may involve a remortgage if you own your home with your ex. 'Make sure you know your housing rights. If you have experienced domestic violence, you can get help from a refuge to leave your home or from a solicitor to get your ex-partner to leave.'

Another legal consideration for all parents, including single parents under any circumstances, is a guardianship plan. This is the legal process of establishing who will step in to care for your children if you're unable to do so for any reason. This can be taken care of at the same time as making your will, which is also something you need to do. Gingerbread charity stresses: 'All newly single parents should update their will or, if they don't have one, write one.'

Making a will doesn't need to be an expensive legal process; you can make one yourself or use an online service that provides an affordable, step-by-step guided process to make things easier. Typically, you register online and someone will call you and talk you through everything, so you'll just have to answer questions on the phone and then get copies signed and stored. This is particularly important if you're separated from your ex-partner but not yet divorced.

Advice for widows and widowers

Gingerbread charity recommends: 'If you are bereaved, you will need to register your partner's death within five days unless the death is reported to the coroner (for example, if the death was unnatural or sudden with no known cause). It is a good idea to buy several copies of the death certificate as you may need to post them to different organisations and it can be expensive to buy more at a later date. You will need to let various government departments know about your bereavement as soon as possible and you can do this using the government's "Tell Us Once" service.

'Finally, you will need to sort out your late partner's estate, i.e. their money, property, possessions and debt. If your late partner has left a will it will explain what should happen to their estate. Dying without a will is known as having died "intestate" and if you are dealing with the estate, you should get legal advice.'

The divorce force

With roughly half of all marriages ending in divorce, family law is big business. Thankfully, the introduction of 'no fault divorce' into UK law has meant a gear change (and relief to a very backed-up court system) and a move away from the blame game or lengthy waits to terminate a marriage. Most couples can now jointly agree that their relationship is no longer tenable due to irreconcilable differences and apply for a divorce. There are still fees involved in this, but they are one-time fees and the process is accessible to all via online forms. Of course, this changes if one party is not agreeable to the divorce, or the terms listed. This is where things can get messy and expensive, especially when solicitors have to take over. Getting through a divorce relatively unscathed is no mean feat. A lot of biting your tongue, thinking before speaking and repeating 'this too shall pass' many times a day helps.

Aside from the marriage itself, the untangling of a life shared requires legal examination too. The dissolution of a marriage draws a line under your union from that point in time, but what came before must be separated as well. When you are married, unless you signed a prenuptial agreement, everything you owned individually until that point becomes a joint possession. Property, cars, shares, savings, even pensions, they all need to be divided upon your separation. Opinion varies on whether you need to get this financial separation legally documented, but it is worth flagging that if you don't make a financial agreement during your divorce, your ex could stake a claim at any point. Your relationship with your ex might be amicable right now, but you can never know what is to come in the future, so spending out on legally protecting your financial separation at this point might be your safest option.

A couple of notes when entering into these negotiations. Unfortunately, as is the case in all areas of life, power is weighted on the side of the rich. If your ex has assets to protect that they don't want to share, they will likely also have access to an expensive solicitor to help them do so. If you are in this situation and don't have the resources to seek legal support, you may be entitled to legal aid. Speak to Citizens Advice or reach out to single-parent charities or abuse charities as appropriate if you need help or support. And above all, remember what is important in all of this. It isn't money. It is your future, for yourself and your children. Does it really matter if your ex walks away with more money? Does it bother you because you need more, or because it is unjust?

Sadly, our world is full of injustices, and dwelling on them is a fast track to unhappiness and bitterness. Your child deserves a parent who is happy. Be really clear and honest with yourself about what you need to survive as a single parent. This should be your goal when it comes to reaching a financial settlement with your ex. You cannot put a price on freedom, but if you could, it would be higher than all the legal fees, stocks, shares and future pension access in the world.

Once you have reached a settlement that works for both of you, the agreement should be signed by both parties and filed with your divorce paperwork. The involvement of a solicitor on at least one side may be advisable here, especially if neither of you has navigated legal matters before, to ensure the settlement is concrete. Once signed, however, your ex can no longer approach you for access to money or insist that their share in a property or car be increased.

Making a house a home

If you owned a house together, this is likely to be the biggest asset to settle on, and if you can acquire sole possession of your family home, this is likely to be the absolute optimum outcome for you and your children, especially if you have majority custody. In a turbulent time, if you can create a safe and stable home for the children, things will be a little easier. If you're in rented accommodation, some legal arrangements will include financial contribution agreements so that you can stay put with financial support from your ex, although it is worth highlighting that these can be very difficult to enforce. If you are the partner moving out of the family home and wondering how you will make a new house into a home, remember that children are inclined to see things as presented by their parents. If you're now living in a smaller house or a flat, where siblings have to share rooms for the first time, or you have less space for indoor play, focusing on the less favourable aspects of your new living arrangements with them is not going to help you, or them. Again, focusing on injustices or looking too far into the future, isn't helpful. Focus on the here and now and what's right in front of you. When you have the children with you, you're in a home filled with love and laughter (make sure there is laughter!) and the kids have a mini holiday every time they're with you. They'll be excited if you make it exciting. And when you're on your own you have the chance to create a home that's exactly as you want it, whether that's set up for work or play. You can now take hour-long bubble baths with nobody knocking on the door. You can stay up all night playing video games without judgement. You might not be in your dream home, but you are free. Focus on the things you need, not on the things you've lost, or think you're owed.

Co-parenting

The legal and financial side of a divorce doesn't actually have to include anything about childcare arrangements. These are typically dealt with separately, since many co-parents have never been married. You do not need a legal arrangement in place to decide on the co-parenting set-up. We will discuss the family court system on page 143, but it is worth pointing out that there is an argument that the only achievement obtained in legalising a childcare arrangement is to attach a financial cost to it. If you have a court-ordered custody arrangement, if either parent breaches the order, you can seek legal recourse or even call the police. But this should always be a last resort. Not only is it expensive to have to seek legal involvement consistently, but also having to involve the police is likely to be distressing for all parties involved, including the children. There are obviously cases where child safety is of concern; you should seek support from your local authority or relevant charities if this is the case, rather than navigating co-parenting on your own.

In most cases, the best option is to reach a co-parenting agreement between you, and stick to it with as much or as little flexibility as works for both of you. You'll have already read some advice on this in Chapter 2, but if you can keep things amicable and the conversation open, everyone will benefit, especially the children. Once you've settled into a routine that works, you should stick to it if you can. If the arrangements no longer work for one or both parties, you will need to renegotiate. This may happen for a number of reasons, including changes to work, a move, a new partner, or changes in childcare or educational settings.

From a legal perspective, having a court-ordered childcare arrangement simply means that these changes may incur legal fees or court-based arguments, not that they can't or won't happen. This is not to say that legally protecting your custody arrangements is never worthwhile, but more that you should think carefully before entering the legal process, because exiting it can be tricky.

Adoption

The agency that you are in contact with regarding the adoption of your child will usually support you through the legal side of the adoption process too. Single adoptive parents will ultimately need an adoption court order to complete the process, which, in effect, permanently severs legal ties between the child and their birth parents. This cannot happen until your child has lived with you for ten weeks. Many families have a celebration day after the court hearing to mark the granting of the adoption order. Once this process is completed, in addition, adoptive parents will need to consider the other legal processes discussed in this chapter's opening, a guardianship plan and a will. If you're separating from the adoptive co-parent of your child, return to the divorce paragraphs above. Family law makes no distinction between biological and adopted children, so the process and challenges will be identical.

So, do you need a lawyer?

If you have ever used a professional legal service, you will know that they are not cheap. Many people go to a solicitor as a default when they are going through a change in situation or having a conflict or custody issue, but there is one thing to ask yourself before you start racking up costs: 'Do I need to pay someone else to have this conversation for me?' To reach the answer to this one, you could try asking a second question: 'Will a lawyer's involvement change the outcome of the conversation?' If the answer to the second question is no, the answer to the first should probably be no, too.

Legal battles often involve astronomical fees because they descend into solicitors sending the other party's solicitor lengthy exchanges that don't go anywhere or achieve anything but are chargeable at incredibly high hourly rates. It is likely that you will need a lawyer or some legal support to complete certain aspects of your single-parent life (such as binding agreements around divorce, bereavement or adoption, as mentioned earlier) but paying for the conversations between parties as to what goes in the documents or agreements is almost always best avoided. The first bill you receive from your solicitor can be a bit of a shock – you'll resent sending work emails for free ever again.

Speaking of these fees, we spoke to Kate Daly, co-founder of divorce service Amicable, whose legal bills got so out of hand that she was inspired to create a business out of her experience. 'I started Amicable after my own train-wreck divorce. My split wasn't amicable, I suffered long-term domestic abuse, so court was perhaps inevitable, but the process almost broke me. It's left me with over a decade of court cases, horrible email and text message exchanges, and a sick feeling in my stomach every time I have to interact with my "other parent". If I could go back in time, I'd tell myself to try to think strategically, not emotionally, and to consider whether fighting for "justice" was really going to best serve my long-term interests.'

One thing to remember when it comes to solicitors is that they are not performing a public service. Law firms are businesses, and they are there to make money. There are legal-aid charities and public legal-advice charities; these are not the same as the private law firms that most people are seeking support (or services) from. Would you ever call a window salesperson and ask them for their opinion on whether you should buy new windows? Or pop in to see a cosmetic surgeon and ask if they thought your nose was straight enough? You get the idea? When you ask a solicitor if they think you need a solicitor, they're probably going to say yes, and send you a bill. Their advice might be good, but it isn't going to be unbiased. They are acting on your behalf, but they are also acting for themselves, because the law is complicated and therefore navigating it is a highly specialised (and lucrative) job. When negotiations between two parties break down, nobody wins, apart from the lawyers. We're not saying that lawyers want negotiations to fail, but if it seems as if they're over-shooting on demands, or your ex is, remember that a quick and easy resolution isn't going to result in the biggest payday for them.

This doesn't mean that knowing your legal options isn't important, however. Kate tells us: 'One of the most important things to establish is a clear understanding about what the law says on how to divide your money and property and sort out arrangements for your children. Traditionally, people go to solicitors, but the trouble with this is, you go to your solicitor and hear your best-case scenario, your ex goes to theirs and hears their best-case scenario and you're left with a big gap to fight over in the middle because you've heard it from a solicitor and you both think your advice is right!'

The alternative is to listen to advice together, by using a service like hers.

Do your homework – set your rule

Being completely clear on what you need from your lawyer in advance is the best way to avoid overpaying or ending up in a never-ending spiral of services and fees. Almost all legal firms offer a complimentary exploratory call in which you can discuss exactly what you need support with; for example, the transfer of your home to one parent, or to create a legally binding financial settlement as part of a divorce proceeding.

If you decide to hire a lawyer, here are some things to consider:

- Ask them to be straight with you on which bits you could or should do yourself (for example, you can fill out and submit all your own divorce forms online and pay directly so that you don't need a solicitor's involvement in the divorce itself at all).
- Ask that you don't correspond over email (as these conversations are chargeable) unless absolutely necessary.
- You can also pre-set spending caps for their work on your case and ask for regular reports on any fees being incurred.
- Simply handing over the legal tasks to a lawyer might be appealing, but doing so is likely to be one of the most expensive mistakes of your single-parent journey.

In a recent poll of Frolo Instagram followers, 77 per cent of those who had been through the legal or family court system since becoming a single parent said that it had been damaging to their mental health. And 90 per cent said that it had cost them more money than they thought it would. Furthermore, only 20 per cent of respondents stated that they thought the system was fair.

It is possible to have a positive experience with your solicitor, and many do. But going into the process with your eyes wide open and knowing what to expect and look out for is always a good idea. If you're worried about money, be very clear with your solicitor that this is the case, and ask that they recommend an alternative if they're unable to help you or think that costs are likely to escalate.

Family court

However much you try to keep things amicable, it takes two. Unfortunately, many cases end up in the family courts. If you are dealing with an abusive ex, drawing out the legal battles might be their last remaining source of power over you, so seek support from domestic-abuse charities if you are going through this, rather than trying to go it alone. It can be helpful to identify in advance if you think your co-parenting relationship could go this way. Kate Daly says: 'In some relationships there are what we call "red flags": behaviours that make it unsafe for you to work cooperatively with your ex. These include where there is domestic abuse, financial abuse, or threats of harm to children. If there are safeguarding issues or drug, alcòhol or addiction issues, you may need the protection of certain court orders and a solicitor to advise and help you with this.'

Some people thrive on the excitement and power of winning a battle with their ex, and for these people, the family court is their chance to show the judge, and the world, that they're right, something that is priceless to them but can be very costly to you and the children. Sadly, if they are charming and persuasive, they might be able to get their way with a judge. For these cases, doing everything you can to limit communication but keeping things amicable and avoiding repeat visits to court will be the best course of action. Read our section on the 'grey rock method' on page 65 if you need a reminder of how to limit escalation in your communications. Again, in these cases it is important to keep in your mind what is really important: do you want to be right, or do you want to be happy? Could you keep a log of every communication you and your ex have ever had, a record of every time they've been late, or a no show, or wronged you and prove to a court that their request for more access or a change of set-up is unjust? Possibly, yes. But is this about what's best for your children, or what is fair, and being proven right? Is the impact that an ongoing court battle is going to have on your mental health, and the knock-on impact on your children worth it? Almost definitely not.

If you're still unsure which path to choose when it comes to navigating child arrangements and/or divorce, this advice from Kate on keeping the long-term picture in mind is key: 'Ultimately, if you have children, you are likely to be in each other's lives, and so thinking about this when you start out on your divorce journey can help you to pick the right process. People often think that the court will hold their ex to account and get them what they think is fair and right, but most people who have been all the way to a final hearing to sort out money and property or who end up in years of Children Act proceedings are broken by the process and bitterly disappointed with the outcome.'

You are, for better or worse, stuck with your co-parent. If you have the option of choosing a path that reduces conflict, the outcome is likely to be better for all parties involved.

Rebecca Giraud and Bob Greig, directors at OnlyMums &

Dads and editors of the book (*Almost*) *Anything but Family Court* by Jo O'Sullivan say: 'Divorce/separation is painful, difficult, and sometimes very complicated, and navigating your way though it well is essential if you are to enjoy the single-parenting years. Avoiding family courts (for those who can) seems to us to be key and the first thing we want to suggest.

'The true cost of going through family court remains hidden. Many parents who have taken this route report the same things to us: a deterioration in their mental health and their bank balance, and anxious children. Almost all report a downturn in their relationship with their ex and their wider family. Such negative outcomes are not quick to resolve. For many, that once-precious relationship with your (now ex) partner can be damaged to the point of no return. We do recognise that for some parents, court is an essential intervention; for many it is not. There are alternatives.

'There are at least 12 different routes that separating couples can take, from mediation, so-called "kitchen table agreements", arbitration and using just one solicitor (a solicitor neutral) to help you work through and reach a reasonable financial settlement and agreements over where the children should be living. There's a clear message running through our book and in all the work we do at OnlyMums & Dads. No matter how daunting and difficult, reaching an agreement with your ex, outside the family courts, that works for both of you will be the best possible outcome for you and your family.'

Right or happy?

Our children's childhoods are so fleeting. Spend every minute of them that you have access to cherishing them. Play with your kids, read to them, hold them. Don't spend so much time fighting for an extra day of access or battling to prove that you're the better parent in the eyes of a judge and then wake up one day to find that this precious time has slipped through your fingers and you've missed it. Never give up fighting for your child's happiness, but do let go of the fight for control. Don't be a pushover or let someone else call the shots, but never lose sight of what is really important: your child's safety and happiness. The only thing we can control is ourselves, and how we treat those around us. Choose kindness and, sometimes, choose biting your tongue. We've asked you this before, and it's time to do it again: do you want to be right? Or do you want to be happy? We choose happiness, every time.

You'll find links to the advice services and relevant information, wherever you are, in our Resources section at the end of this book.

My single-parent story

*James Hunt, co-parent to two autistic sons,
@storiesaboutautism on Instagram and
storiesaboutautism.com*

My story always feels as if it's a little bit unique, there are not many who I've found to have exactly the same circumstances. My ex-wife and I separated six years ago and we have two boys who are both autistic, with quite a high level of support needs. For about two or three years before that, our boys were really struggling around each other. Jude is very noise sensitive, he doesn't like unpredictable behaviour, and his younger brother Tommy, unfortunately, was everything in the world that he didn't like. So, we found that we were naturally having to separate them and we just fell into that rhythm.

When we got to the point of separating, Jude had had a long period of self-harming and meltdowns, and that overtook everything. Whatever we were going through relationship-wise, the emotions we were trying to deal with, when your child's self-harming, it's something that just takes over. Then we came to the realisation that we were separating. We thought: 'How could one of us have both the boys at the same time?' We came to the decision that we would take one boy each and we would swap over every couple of days, whatever fit in with the routines.

It's quite a different single-parent experience, almost as if you're a lone single parent, because you've always got a child. At the same time, there is the other parent, who's also doing the same as you. It was a temporary thing, which turned out to be the best thing we could have done. Both boys are much happier. They've developed a lot in the last few years. And we're coming to a stage where we're starting to integrate them together, and it's working. All relationships that end are hard, but at least we could see that the boys were happier.

In those early days it was very overwhelming; it felt like too much. Sometimes I think you just have to slow down, and accept that it's going to be a tough time for a few months. But it will get better. And you will find a way to cope with it.

James's advice

Tommy and Jude have definitely taught me about enjoying life, about making the most of life. Naturally I'm an over-thinker, and they've somehow taught me to be less of that, to live in the moment. Most of us take for granted what we assume life is going to be like, and we grow up expecting life to go a certain way. We've watched films and TV shows and books, and we plan how happy life is going to be. And then it feels like it's all falling apart. It's about realising that it can still be OK, you can still have a life, very different from what you expected, but it can still be a very fun and very happy life. That doesn't mean it won't be hard – it doesn't mean there won't be hard moments.

I'm proud of how we've all coped with what we've been through. I didn't think that I'd be talking about autism, talking about being a parent. That was never something that I thought would be my thing. But it's probably the best thing I've ever done. And it's saved me many times, and hopefully, it's helping others too.

7

Shake it Off – Banishing the Single-/Solo-parent Stigma

'When we unpack our internalised messages, we can choose to update our attitudes and open ourselves to fresh possibilities, but change is threatening, even when it's the best possible choice.'

Psychotherapist Charlotte Fox Weber

Once you've worked out a few of the practicalities of raising a family alone and steadying your little ship, shaking off the single-parent stigma can be one of the hardest remaining hurdles for newly single parents. Hopefully, as you're working through this book you'll be feeling more empowered and less 'labelled' in your role, but ideally you'll reach a place where you can celebrate, rather than just accept, your status as a solo head of a family. If, when you hear the term 'single mum' or 'single dad', 'solo parent' or 'widower', you immediately think of strong, empowered individuals doing two jobs and generally smashing it, you can proceed to the next chapter (please pass 'go' and collect £200 on the way – Monopoly money only, we're single parents after all). If, however, you hear the words 'single parent' and immediately feel sad, judgemental, angry or ashamed, we've got a tiny bit of work to do in this chapter. Like the rest of this book, though, it's going to be a hoot, so hang around.

Why the stigma?

Let's try to get to the bottom of where this single-parent stigma is coming from, shall we? Historically, the media hasn't done us any favours. Portraits of fictional single mums on TV and in films are often of chaotic and promiscuous women who are usually drinking a lot. Single dads on screen (seemingly only ever portrayed as widowers) are adorable but overwhelmed, ready to be rescued, emotionally, by a woman.

There is an undeniable difference in the tone of how mums and dads going it alone are portrayed, however. James Hunt (@storiesaboutautism) told us: 'On a public perception, we're pretty lucky as single dads. I don't have to do a lot to be praised. I get a fraction of the hate that single mums get, or mums who post on social media get. I could do something that mums do every single day, and I get "Oh, what an amazing dad." And mums don't get told that they're an amazing mum. I'm very aware of that.'

But on the flipside, there can be less support out there for single dads too, so finding connection and like-minded parents to help you find your feet can be a challenge. 'I'd like to see a bigger community of the dads that are out there reaching out and being a bit more supportive of each other,' says James. As we'll cover in the next section, single mums tend to get somewhat of a tougher ride when it comes to representation.

Single parents on screen from almost all walks of life are presented as half of a whole, just waiting for the other piece to come back or a new piece to come along and fill the void. Let's not even go there with the minority or niche solo parent set-ups and their portrayal, because there isn't any. The portraits of real-life single parents tell a different story. We're thinking *Erin Brokovich* (portrayed by the practically perfect Julia Roberts), an unemployed single mum of three who took on energy giants PG&E and won. We're thinking Chris Gardner, a single dad who experienced periods of homelessness with a toddler son who went on to become a successful stockbroker with his own firm and the subject of *The Pursuit Of Happyness* film, starring Will Smith. The constructed narratives are plentiful and can become ingrained, but we urge you to look to the latter. Look to the true stories. Yes, there are struggles, but there are triumphs. There is love. We believe that every single parent is an Erin Brokovich or a Chris Gardner waiting to happen. (Hell, let's take some time out at this juncture to watch both films back to back before reconvening.)

Destitution, desperation

Let's veer off-screen shall we, and into the papers. Single parents, and more frequently single mums, get a lot of press. But before you start celebrating this representation win, try giving the words a little google and see what your news feed offers you. All too often, it's tragic tales of adversity, frequently accompanied by the words 'broke', 'helpless' and 'desperate'.

One former UK prime minister even described the children of single mothers as 'ill-raised, ignorant, aggressive and illegitimate' in a column, despite having left a string of single mother exes in his wake. (The narrative of the single parent has all too frequently been that of one to be pitied, shamed, judged or ridiculed. We get it, bad news sells, but this is frequently the case in which single parents, specifically mums, are mentioned in 'positive' stories, too. Success stories cite single parenthood as something that has been 'overcome' or 'endured'.

There are lots of stories that carry the headline 'From Single Mum to [insert literally anything else]'. The suggestion here is that starting out as a 'single mum' is literally the worst possible start, and achieving anything from such a low starting position would be a win. Imagine flipping these headlines on their, ahem, heads. 'From Unhappily Married to Single Mum!' 'From Dreaming of Having a Family to Being a Single Mum!' (The fact that nobody is selling this story is one of the reasons we wrote this book: this is it.)

Single parenthood as a named circumstance in itself all too often carries the assumption of negativity. Single-parent prefixes tend only to be applied where they can cause surprise or reaffirm negative stereotypes. 'Single mum can't afford to feed her family' or 'Single mum wins big on the lottery', never 'Single dad directs yet another award-winning series' or 'Single mum scores winning goal in big match'. Even if the explicitly negative weight isn't attached to the single-parent label as an inclusion, the audience is already trained to add it, due to our social conditioning and pre-existing assumptions regarding single-parent stigma. As a single parent, particularly a new one, this can all lead to a whole lot of insecurity about how you are now living your life, and how others will now be perceiving you. This can lead to feelings of anxiety or low self-esteem, which will not only get in the way of your parenting, but also in the way of embracing this exciting new opportunity to rewrite your life story, starting right now. That's why it's so important that we recognise where these feelings are coming from, because the roots are fictional, not actual. We can therefore make a conscious choice to override them.

Broken home

How many times have you heard the phrase 'broken home' to describe children from single-parent households? The term is most commonly applied specifically to single-parent households that are the result of a marriage that has been dissolved, or 'broken' down, but it's such a blanket phrase that it is often applied to any children who don't come from the traditional nuclear family set-up. If you are a single parent following the breakdown of a marriage, please allow us to tell you, once and for all, that your home is not broken. Your marriage may have been, but your home is not. Your marriage might have been broken beyond repair, but your home is not. Your marriage may, in fact, have been what was breaking your home. Your marriage may have been the thing bringing conflict, instability, unhappiness and uncertainty into your and your children's lives, and by removing the marriage from your home, you may, in fact, have fixed it. Both parties in your marriage may now go on and build happy, fixed homes of their own and provide safe, secure environments for their kids to thrive in.

Single-parent homes can be safe, they can be secure, they can be warm and happy and full of love and laughter. They can contain absolutely everything that children need to thrive. What, about that, is 'broken'? The language is what is broken. It is the system that leaves parents with endless hurdles to navigate and single parents without anyone to help or support them when overcoming them: *that* is broken.

There is nothing broken about our homes.

'I'm sorry'

Above and beyond the explicit single-parent stereotypes are all the implied ones. The unwritten weights that singledom and its attached associations carry. Divorce, death, adultery, abuse or being generally unlovable: the tragedy, drama or just plain old lack of commitment that led to our single-parent status. Single parenthood is so frequently painted in a negative light that often when you tell someone you're a single parent they react with 'I'm sorry'. They are immediately picturing the array of dreadful things that must have happened to lead you to such a terrible circumstance. Of course, sometimes it is terrible things that led you here. If it is, we really *are* sorry. But the assumption of terrible things being the only reason you could endure such an existence? Nope. No thank you. Audacious, unbelievable, disrespectful, uncouth, unnecessary. Imagine telling someone, 'I live in Basingstoke' and them replying with 'I'm sorry'. Or someone telling you, 'I just got engaged' and you replying with 'I'm sorry'. One might argue that either one would be more natural reasons for condolences. (Only joking, Basingstoke is lovely.)

You shouldn't be sorry

We're not sorry to be single parents. We're not sorry that day in, day out, we do the job of two parents at once. We're not sorry that we get to rewrite the rules of what a happy family looks like, that we have the privilege of raising children whose needs are fulfilled and who have all the love they need.

We are not sorry, and you shouldn't be either. But how do we get you here? How can we overcome this single-parent stigma and turn it into pride in your position? Identifying the route of it is important. We've already covered where some of the negative stereotypes come from, but why does that resonate with you? Often, perceived stigma may be internalised shame. In the case of single parenthood this might be the result of diverting from the course laid out to us over and over, in books, on TV, in Disney films and even by the laws and policies benefitting nuclear family set-ups: girl meets boy, they fall in love, get married, have a baby, live happily ever after. Anything other is a misstep or a failure. At one point in the narrative (or maybe even more if you've chosen to have a baby alone, ditched the marriage step or are from the queer community) you've strayed from the safe and secure game of life that we're all sold from a young age. This perceived 'failure' can lead to shame, which, when internalised and unexamined, can lead to perceived stigma. Since the 'right way' of being a parent has been shown to us over and over again from a very early age, it's time to make the unconscious bias against single-parent families conscious.

Is the worst stigma you're experiencing coming from others, or from yourself? Are you subconsciously hiding your single-parent status from others? Do you add caveats when you do disclose it? Is this because of how you think other people will feel about it, or how *you* feel about it, deep down? 'Ask yourself where your judgements come from,' says psychotherapist Charlotte Fox Weber. 'Whose voice is telling you that single parenting is somehow shameful or suboptimal? Where did you learn this story? When you understand where your internal scripts come from, personally and culturally, you can rewrite the narrative. Have compassion for the part of you that feels stigmatised. Outgrowing old scripts is liberating and empowering, but it's also daunting at moments. You might feel feisty and free one minute, and insecure and marginalised the next. It's all part of healing, including the pain of reopened wounds.'

'Embracing the challenge is how we grow and expand,' says Charlotte. 'It can be joyous to change your mind about an issue, to shift a view, even in subtle ways. Notice the way your views have changed, and continue to free yourself from rigid outlooks. Narrow and stale attitudes towards family make "sheeple" out of people. It's threatening to many when someone breaks the predictable pattern, and single parenting challenges people in all sorts of ways. Those who judge it and make assumptions are coming from a place of fear. Continue to update your story and talk openly with people who show curiosity and respect. It's not your job to explain your situation to the world, but find the people who understand and who are interested in forward motions.'

Feelings of guilt or shame are really common in the early days of single parenthood, but if you're able to identify what it is that is causing the guilt or shame, you'll be one step closer to overcoming it. Understanding that you likely feel guilty for straying from a path that was never meant for you in the first place isn't easy; however, you'll soon realise that people have been taking shortcuts, veering off-piste, hitch-hiking, looping back around to start again or just taking another route entirely and reaching the destination of 'happily ever after' in a myriad of different ways and at a range of different speeds all around you, you just didn't notice until you were one of them. Think back to your childhood. Were every single one of your friends raised by two happy parents in a happy home? Were any of them? Were you? We all knew kids whose parents were divorced, widowed, foster carers, who were adopted, had step-parents, lived in blended families, were raised by a grandparent, an aunt or an uncle. Some of us were those kids. But still, when we hear 'family' we picture a mum, a dad and two or three children. Catch yourself in these thoughts, remember your own higgledy-piggledy family or those of your friends, full of love and laughter and chaos, and everything that family life entails. These families are just as valid as the nuclear ones we've all grown up seeing represented as the norm.

Stigma vs discrimination

You are allowed to feel that single parenting is hard. It is. But try to remember that it is hard for other parents too, for lots of reasons. Be aware of alternative 'otherisms' that are impacting the parents around you, some in very obvious and challenging ways. As a single parent, you might feel as if you're not like the families you see around you, but remember that all sorts of parents are navigating the spaces around them and feeling like outsiders too – many in a much more visible way. Parents living with disabilities or neurodiversity, parents who are in the minority due to their race, heritage, socio-economic status, age, sexuality or religion. The school drop-off can feel like reverting to our school years ourselves, worried about fitting in and being judged by those around us.

Leon Wenham is a black, gay, solo adopter, and his single-parent status wasn't on his mind at the school gates, but his gender, race and sexuality, was. 'I was conscious of it, initially. I wondered if they would know that I'm gay, or if they'd just see a black male, not knowing if I was straight or not. Some of the school mums weren't overly friendly at first, I would smile of course, but I was wondering: *Do they think I'm trying to crack on to them?* I was thinking: *Baby, you're not my type, so it's all good!* You can see the curiosity, the questions forming.'

Whatever stigma or discrimination you're feeling the weight of when it comes to parenting, how do you get over it? The first step is working on feeling comfortable and confident within yourself. Leon puts this beautifully: 'I was conscious of it. But I didn't feel self-conscious about it.'

If in doubt, a good rule of thumb to follow is 'it's not about you'. Harsh as it sounds, humans are all walking around in their own worlds with their own problems to navigate. They're probably not thinking about you at all.

Charlotte Fox Weber says that self-acceptance is the key to coming to terms with your new situation. 'Self-acceptance is a superpower. Assume that others will make assumptions and get things wrong about you – we all do – but it's golden to be able to tolerate misunderstandings and have clarity from within so that you don't feel pushed to prove yourself to everyone you encounter. When you understand your own perspective, you have a better chance of articulating issues to others, if you want to convey what matters to you.'

However, it's equally important not to feel as if you have to justify your life or choices to others too. Charlotte says: 'You may be finding your own individual path and people looking in at your life might not understand each and every move you make. Be gentle with yourself. You may crave a sense of belonging, and yet stepping off the trodden path evokes feelings of disconnection, even alienation. Not fitting into the usual group is a courageous and wonderful thing, and there are others out there who get it. Normalise the moments of isolation and keep yourself open to new connections.'

We are all single parents

One final note on an additional issue that really feeds into the stigmatisation of single and solo parents: much of the shaming that single parents face comes from within the parenting community. It comes from feeling misunderstood or labelled, and mostly it comes from a lack of understanding about the nuances of solo or single-parent life. There are multiple threads online about what exactly constitutes being a single parent. About whether 50/50 co-parents are worthy of the 'single parent' title, when they have another, absent parent contributing from afar and 50 per cent of their time alone. About how some single or solo parents have financial support from an ex, large support networks around them, or move in with family to help, and whether that somehow belittles or negates their lone parent status.

Every co-parent has been told by a married friend how 'lucky' they are that they get nights off from their child or children, while they are 'stuck at home 24/7' with their family. (On this, let us please clarify once and for all to all the cohabiting parents: either one of you can leave the house literally any time you want, as long as the other parent is there. If you run out of milk and need an evening cuppa or, even worse, loo roll, once the kids are in bed, you can pop to the shop while your kids are safe with your partner at home with them. A last-minute invite to a work event comes in: you can say yes, because you have no strictly enforced childcare schedule to adhere to. You get the idea?) We have all listened to people refer to themselves as 'practically a single parent' every time their partner goes away on a trip.

These bugbears aside, trying to compete with other single or solo parents for who is most worthy of the title is completely counter-intuitive. If you buy into these arguments, instead of finding solace and closeness in our diverse and glorious single-parent community, you are further isolating yourself. Yes, co-parents typically have some of their childcare needs fulfilled, but many are having to co-parent with an abuser, causing unimaginable trauma or anxiety that remains ongoing. Others have the person who cheated on them, someone unreliable or unhelpful, as their 'teammate'. They are often navigating conflicting parenting ideologies and trying to make a child who lives between two homes feel settled and supported. Some face ongoing battles over child-maintenance payments, custody agreements or minor day-to-day struggles such as trying to get a lost coat returned from their ex. Most of them wish they could have their children at home full-time, and hate saying goodbye to them each and every time they have to. Many feel shame that they aren't able to have their kids at home full-time, that they've failed in some way by not being there for 100 per cent of their kids' childhoods.

Meanwhile, lone parents often have nobody to contribute to costs and nobody to call on for regular childcare without shelling out for professional childcare. Widows and widowers are navigating their and their children's grief as well as adjusting to this challenging new world of lone parenting. Some single parents face other challenges day to day – disabilities, neurodiversities, discrimination or financial hardships – that make the single-parent stigma pale in comparison. Despite all the nuances of single, solo and co-parenting life, one thing unites us all: we are all raising children alone, whether full- or part-time. We all have to make impossibly difficult decisions alone. We have to keep on top of multiple schedules, school runs, childcare costs, meal plans, bills and routines without a partner to share the load with. We are all full-time single parents mentally, even if not physically. We are all in this together. We are all doing our best, and getting better with every day that passes.

James Hunt agrees that avoiding the single-parent-hardship Olympics is wise: 'There is always a sense of "your life is more difficult than my life" or "I don't get as much time",' he says. 'And I sometimes look on with jealousy as other single parents have lots of free time, but then I also know single parents who really struggle with that free time, because they miss their kids. My set-up is very different [having one of my two boys living with me at any given time], but I get to see one of my boys every day. And obviously, there're dads who see their kids only every other weekend. And I couldn't imagine going through that. I mean, perhaps I wouldn't mind half the time off every now and again! But I've seen friends who are torn apart every time that happens. It's about the whole, rather than the individual circumstances.'

Things not to say to a single parent

We wish we could distribute these lists to the non-single parent community.

- I don't know how you do it! I couldn't cope.
- My partner is always at work so I'm basically a single parent.
- You're so lucky you get time off when your kids are at their other parent's!
- Your children are doing so well despite being from a broken home.
- Don't worry, you'll meet someone else.
- You must get benefits or child maintenance, right?

Things to say to a single parent, instead

- Can I help or support you in any way?
- My partner is away, why don't you come over to hang out with us?

- It must be hard being away from the kids, I hope you get a chance to recharge.
- Your kids are amazing.
- You're doing an incredible job.
- I have so much respect for all that you manage, alone.

Single-parent pride

Once you're feeling proud of your single-parent status, any perceived stigma will fall away, and only the actual stereotyping, micro-aggressions and occasional downright rudeness will remain. Preparing preferred retorts to some of the classics will give you peace of mind and provide entertainment. These can come in a range of forms. There's classic sarcasm ('Isn't it hard being a single parent?' – 'Not for me, I'm brilliant'), bluntness ('Doesn't he need his dad at home?' – 'Not as much as you need new manners'), disorientation ('I don't know how you do it' – 'I don't ') or the truth ('Aren't you lonely?' – 'Only when I'm away from my kids, but getting them all to myself at other times makes up for it').

SIDENOTE Giving the finger in any or all of these instances is also fine. People will continually make comments that irritate or upset you. From the digs levelled at single folks around the globe ('You'll meet someone else soon' or 'Don't give up on love') to thoughtless throwaway comments that you'll find yourself replaying days later ('Perhaps you'll get it right next time' or 'I'd never break up my home'). If someone catches you on a bad day with one of these sucker punches, it could feel as if it's enough to sink the ship, but we'll let you in on a little secret here: your kids are the emergency flotation devices you never knew you needed. On the days where it's impossibly hard, they will motivate you to carry on. Their love, and your love for them, will keep you afloat. But it's infinitely easier to stay buoyant if you're feeling buoyant about your single-parenting situation. We promise you it's worth putting in the effort here.

Find inspiration

On this note, if you're not ready to uphold yourself as the picture of single-parent pride just yet (you will be soon, we promise), find people doing the job that you respect and look to them, instead. Find single parents, of all types, on social media who have their shit together, and be inspired by their success (no doom-scrolling or comparing and despairing though, promise us, or we're confiscating your phones). Watch *The Pursuit Of Happyness* one more time – it really is very good. If you were raised by a single parent who made you feel loved and supported, look to them. Aren't you proud of the job they did? You'll be proud of the job you do too.

Single-parent pride is powerful, but like all true pride it must be earned. Once you've reframed what your idea of 'family' is and addressed any shame or guilt hangovers, you'll begin to accept your single-parent status and the perceived stigma will start to shrink. With acceptance comes empowerment, the confidence that what you're doing is not only OK, but it's extraordinary. Little by little, you will start to feel proud of what you're achieving, what you're doing day in, day out, all by yourself. The decisions you're making, the steps forward you're taking, building a solid foundation for your future and your child's.

Fake it till you make it

If you're still feeling a little shaky about the whole single-parent title, we promise you that it won't be for ever. This one really is a 'fake it till you make it' situation. Before long you'll find yourself announcing to strangers that you're a single parent and expecting a round of applause. We should warn you, one won't always be forthcoming, but you won't really need it anyway. Once you've shaken off your own single-parent stigma, you'll be ready to talk to the children about their home life in helpful, constructive and positive ways. There's no right or wrong way to address your home set-up with your kids. Finding diverse books, TV programmes and video games for them to engage with that show not only a range of different children but also different home set-ups will be helpful. Remember that as abnormal as your home set-up might feel to you at times, we get to teach our kids what normal is. If you're a solo parent or you've been a single parent since the kids were small, they'll grow up finding their home life to be positively ordinary (no offence). If you separated from your children's other parent slightly later in life, the kids might need your guidance in getting used to their new life. This is why it's so important to prioritise overcoming any lurking internalised stigma so that you don't pass this along to your kids. Our job as parents is to make sure our children feel safe, secure and loved.

Being positive

Let's try a little exercise to help banish any niggles of single-parent stigma and provide a framework for a more positive view in this area, shall we?

1. Firstly, list five single parents whom you respect or look up to. They don't have to be ones you know in real life.

2. Now, list five people who were raised by single parents that have turned out to be happy, successful, well-adjusted adults (and not ill-raised, ignorant, aggressive and illegitimate as per that earlier comment).

3. If you're not ready to big up your solo- or single-parent status just yet, think of these role models in the first list and let them motivate you. And remember that your kids have every opportunity to thrive in the world under your guidance, just like those in the second list.

4. Now, write down everything you think of when you hear the words 'single parent', 'single or solo mum' or 'single or solo dad'. Circle any that you think apply to you.
   Are the words you've circled positive or negative? Think about why you've picked these words, and whether they reflect your feelings or other people's.

5. Finally, write three ways that you want to introduce yourself as a single or solo parent to others going forward. Of course, you have no obligation to disclose anything to others about your set-up, but it's helpful to have phrases that you're comfortable with ready to go. Make sure the words you pick are positive, that they don't involve caveats or assumptions of a negative bias. Here are a few for inspiration: to bring up the topic with school-parent friends around the holidays: 'It's just me and my little boy at home, so we are always going on adventures together.' In work situations: 'I'm a single parent, so my organisational skills are second to none.' On a date: 'I'm a single parent, so I have very high standards!'

Turning single-parent stigma into pride is about turning self-doubt into self-confidence, which will take time, but single-parenting time runs incredibly fast (unless it's that last hour before bedtime), so you'll be singing your solo status from the rooftops before you know it.

8

We'll Be There for You – Making Friends

'As single parents, it's important to feel connected and supported, not only for ourselves but so we can be the best versions of ourselves for our kids.'

Zoë, on founding Frolo

What is the first rule of single-parent club? We *do* talk about single-parent club. Making single-parent friends is just about the best part of riding solo. We have both been part of a WhatsApp group of single mums for about three years now, and although we don't get to all meet up very often (there are 37 of us) the group is one of the most active chats on our phones. The group is diverse in terms of age, race, wealth, sexuality and situation, but the one common thread of single parenthood is enough to tie us all together and keep the support line open all hours year after year. There are conversations about co-parenting, legal matters, finances and other single-parent issues, but there is also culture, fashion, sex and memes a-plenty too. Among the group there have been camping trips, festival meetups, joint Christmases, remarriages and new babies. Our lives are richer for being a part of the single-parent community, and while you might not feel like it at this moment, your life is about to get richer too. This chapter is all about finding your new place in the world, and the friends that you'll need to settle you in.

Loneliness

We've touched on loneliness in several chapters of this book and pointed out that single parents are rarely alone for long (the 'parent' part of the title takes care of that); however, we don't want to downplay the very real issue of loneliness for single parents, particularly those that are new to single parenthood and going through an adjustment in circumstances. Loneliness carries health risks, with studies linking loneliness to an increased risk of heart disease, stroke, obesity, depression, stress and anxiety, with links to overall morbidity and mortality in adults.[*] We don't include this to scare you, but to reassure you that you are allowed to take these feelings seriously.

Being lonely isn't just about living alone. You can be in a crowd of people and still feel completely alone. When you go through a big change, it can feel like your old sources of comfort and companionship have disappeared, and this can leave you feeling lost and lonely. When you put the kids to bed in the evening and you are stuck in a quiet house, you might feel lonely, despite not being home alone. Psychotherapist Charlotte Fox Weber, author of *What We Want*, says: 'Let yourself lean when you can. When you feel utterly alone, admit it to someone, even if it's just to yourself. Say it aloud. It's human and survivable, and you can pat yourself on the back. Encouragement and connection are the biggest sources

* Yanguas J., Pinazo-Henandis S., Tarazona-Santabalbina F.J., 'The complexity of loneliness', *Acta Biomed*, 2018 (Jun 7);89(2):302–314. doi: 10.23750/abm.v89i2.7404. PMID: 29957768; PMCID: PMC6179015.

of vitality, and when you look for it, there are surprising pos-sibilities.' Finding connection to get you through these lonely times is not only possible, but it is also necessary. And that is where the single-parent community comes in.

When one door closes

Being open to making new friends, at any time of life, is a truly wonderful thing. Becoming a single parent can feel as if it's all about loss: the loss of a partner, the loss of the life you thought you had; loss of joint friendships; loss of friends who just don't have the patience for what you're going through; loss of in-laws and extended family groups. It is easy to get lost in all this loss and lose sight (yet another loss!) of the space this is creating for new friendships and relationships. We're not saying that the grief of these losses isn't valid; it *is* valid and it is important to acknowledge and feel it, but try to be mindful of the opportunity for growth and change here too. You might not be ready just yet. But when you are, as the grief for your life as it was becomes a little more bearable, being open to letting the light back in, to adding to your circle of friends and family, is absolutely vital. Nobody knows this better than Zoë, who took this longing for a new light in her life post-split and turned it into a business all about bringing single parents together.

The birth of Frolo

I (Zoë) was inspired to create Frolo as a result of the struggle and feelings of loneliness, isolation and 'otherness' that I experienced when I became a single parent. I searched high and low for a way to find other single parents like me, and for the community and connection I needed at the time, and when I realised it didn't exist, I decided to create the solution myself.

That solution was an app just for single parents that would make it easy to discover and connect with other local like-minded single parents so that I could make friends that could relate to what I was going through, and organise playdates with people like me, who had kids the same age. I also wanted to be able to seek guidance and support about certain things I was dealing with as a single parent, so I wanted a way to connect with a wider community too. Then I thought of being able to find and organise meetups, playdates, holidays, and nights out with ease, so I envisioned a meetup section too. And a chat section, where I could message my connections, or have group chats with single parents in my area, or those I had shared interests with or similar parenting experiences with. And, of course, I thought about safety, because my ideal solution was an app experience that was positive and empowering, plus safe to use.

And so, in 2019, the Frolo (friends plus solo – my attempt at a more positive rebrand of the term 'single parents') app was brought to life and launched.

The Frolo Community has completely changed my life. It has given me best friends and extended family; it has given me full, fun weekends that I don't wish away. It has given me so many happy experiences and memories, holidays and laughs, it has given me support and understanding in my low moments from people who truly understand and can empathise. It has given me the reassurance that my son shouldn't feel othered or less-than for growing up in a single-parent household. It has flipped on its head completely the narrative in my mind of what it means to be a single parent and how society perceives single parents. Now, I could not feel more proud of being a single parent or more grateful for the support network of friends and the richness of life it has opened up to me, *because* of being a single parent. And my non-single parent friends often tell me that they have Frolo FOMO because of the amazing friendships, connections and experiences I get to have because of Frolo and being a single parent.

I am proud to say that the Frolo Community is changing lives with users referring to it as a lifeline. One frolo dad recently stated that using Frolo Community daily is a crucial part of his mental-health hygiene. Already, the Frolo Community has seen over 500k connections between single parents and over 2 million in-app messages sent. Once you've downloaded the app and signed up, select Community Mode and introduce yourself on the Feed tab (where you'll receive a warm welcome!), search for Frolos in your area and use the Meetup tab to find out what's happening online or near you, or get involved in one of the many Group Chats that cover all areas of single-parent life.

Not just single mums

There can be a feeling within the single-parent community that it's only single mums that need support. But one in ten single-parent families is headed by a man, and countless more men have co-parenting responsibilities. We believe that all of them would benefit from support from those in the same situation.

Co-parent and former footballer Jamie Redknapp told us: 'I discovered Frolo when I became a single dad. There was a lot of guidance in there, lots of questions that were hard to answer, and you could get all the advice you wanted from the app. And I'm not ashamed to say that I used the Frolo Community and found it very helpful. It's not for just women, it's not just for men, it's for everybody. And whether it's your first child or your third, and even now I've got a new baby with my new partner, I'm still learning every single day, as they're all so different. I think it's important for both single mums and dads to be able to access the community and support.'

You win some, you lose some

When you become a single parent, you might look around at your married parent friends or childless friends and suddenly feel that you don't have anything in common with them. They might be willing to listen, but you might feel that nobody can relate to what you're going through. All single parents lose friends along the way. You might find it hard to be around traditional family units if you're post-split or grieving, or you might feel isolated from your single friends who seem to have a lot more freedom. Do you remember the old adage about relationships being for a reason, a season or a lifetime? Becoming a single parent is a good time to find out which of those your current friendships sit within. If you haven't been in this situation yourself, and you're a bit naff at empathy, you might not have the patience or generosity to remain friends with a single parent. Thank you. Next! There are plenty more fish in the sea, and you're now swimming in a sea rich in capable, strong, independent, diverse, unique, mad, sad, glad, bad and (mostly) rad fellow single parents. Make friends with some of them.

They're just like me

The first friends you'll need when you become a single parent are fellow divorcees, widowers, solo parents and adopters: parents doing the job of two people at once. We've already spoken about how, although we might all be in different situations, there is more bringing us together than dividing us. Single parents just innately 'get it', even if they're navigating different circumstances than you are. Having said that, if you can find people in exactly the same situation as you, it can be a truly glorious thing. Finding someone who has just become a single parent via exactly the same set of circumstances who lives in your vicinity might be slightly unlikely (although not impossible). That is where the Internet comes into play. Social media is a great place to find people in your position with whom you can connect or look to for advice. The real lifesavers of the single-parent friendship pool are the ones going through the same thing at the same time as you are: the single dad trying to fight for more access to their children; the bereaved single mum navigating grief and becoming the solo head of a household; the solo adopter with a million questions and a lot of doubt.

You'll feel a hell of a lot less alone once you know that there are other people out there doing exactly what you're doing, at exactly the same time. On spaces such as the Frolo app you'll not only find thousands of single parents, but also groups of parents in exactly your situation. The comfort that you can find from connecting with these groups is absolutely priceless.

James Hunt (@storiesaboutautism) says: 'I felt very alone those first few years [after becoming a single parent]. I didn't know anybody whose children were autistic; I didn't really know anything about autism. It's only when you go on a course, or you go online and find people to surround yourself with, that you suddenly realise: of course there's thousands of people out there who are going through exactly what you're going through and have already been through it. Through my blog I was building up a community of people to turn to, to talk to about autism, about all the challenges and the good times. So I would definitely recommend for people in the same situation to just start online and search out pages like mine or others out there. Start building your community.'

In addition to the plethora of online single-parent friends that can make you feel seen, heard and held, having some local single parents to connect with is all kinds of wonderful. Not only can you get the kids together and have coffee (or wine) while they play, and talk about all the joys and hardships of parenting, but you can also form a support network for each other that will stop you from ever feeling alone again. Spaces such as the Frolo app can help with this: you can meet other single parents in your area and attend local meetups to connect with like-minded people, even searching to find people with kids the same age as yours.

Advice for solo adopters

The following advice comes from adoption advocate, Leon Wenham (@lots_andlotsoflove):

Create a safe space for questions

It's really important for my son to know that our home is a safe space, so that he can ask me questions about his adoption and his life story. He often asks questions, and we've got lots of photo albums and memory boxes from his previous foster carers. As he's older, I will continue to give more information.

Initially, he would say, 'I want a real family' or a 'normal family'. And I obviously had to do a lot of work around different families. We have lots of books, and I give him examples of different families that we know. He knows I'm gay. He knows what that means. He's been to pride with me; he's absolutely cool. Initially, when he said, 'I just want a mum,' I said, 'Well, you do have a mum, but she doesn't live with you.' Then he says, 'I want a mum in the same house' to which I would say, 'I'm gay, so, it's not gonna happen.' Then it's, 'So why don't you get a boyfriend, get married and I'll have two dads then?!' I think if kids are asking, they're ready to hear it.

Tips for transracial adopters

Do the work. You have to do the work. And it's a lifetime commitment. It's not just a case of reading a couple of books, or familiarising yourself with a local Caribbean or Indian takeaway, it's about pushing through your own discomfort. Because having a child of colour, as a non-black person, doesn't absolve you of racism, prejudice or unconscious bias or conscious bias. I've spoken to a lot of white parents that have transracially adopted; they're not comfortable in majority black spaces, they aren't even comfortable delving into the heritage and the background of that child.

I believe this is really problematic, because you're adding that layer of confusion around their identity, and adopted children have that anyway. A lot of adoptees can suffer from impostor syndrome, I am under no illusion, no matter how amazing I make my child's upbringing, I'm never going to be his birth mum, I'm never going to give him what he feels like he's lacking. I can give him as much love and as many experiences as possible. But I can't fill that void, and I know that. So add on to that a further lack of identity or not looking like anybody in your family, not feeling comfortable to discuss or ask questions, is problematic. So I think doing the work expanding your network that reflects your child's background, visiting the country of origin, and trying to find groups within that community, you have to proactively do that. You can't just think love is enough, because it's not.

Remember, however, that you are enough

I've got a balance of masculine and feminine energy. Being super-attentive is usually linked to the role of a mother, and being a bit firmer the father; however, I quite easily do both. It feels comfortable to me. I know that my son sees and appreciates that, as well. Initially, I thought: *Does he need a mother's love, or the nurturer?*, but I can give him all that, and I'm conscious that I do.

You might not have time to date, for a while

I just don't have the respite. The reality is, I'm busy. I aspire to have a courtship, cinema dates, Columbia Road flower market on a Sunday, but the reality is, until I get to the stage when my son can be included, who's going to look after my child while I get to know somebody?

Adopting an older child from the care system

There's no rule book. Sometimes, during the training process, there's a massive focus on therapeutic parenting. The reality is: all children are different. If they've had multiple homes, each home that they've lived in will have had a different approach to parenting. Do what works for you and your family. Be mindful of the trauma and the background and the unpicking that you have to do. I appreciate his adoption and understand adoption trauma, but boundaries are important, and adopted children need and crave boundaries, it makes them feel safe.

Listen to people's advice, solicited or otherwise, but the reality is that you need to do whatever works for you in your home.

Look after yourself

I am a big advocate for self-care. Personally, I love a facial. Love a pedicure.

They just like me

The second lot of friends you'll need as a single parent are just any old Tom, Dick or Harriet who will understand your situation and gladly pick up the pieces (or your child from school) when you take a tumble. In the early days of single parenthood, being friends with single and solo parents is easier because you're finding your feet and don't want to measure yourself against others or see yourself through their eyes until you get used to your new reflection. But once you're settled into single-parent life and you have a pool of friends in a similar situation (whether local or online), it's time to cast the net a little wider. Honestly, when it comes to parenting, the 'it takes a village' adage is completely accurate. The more people you can move into your village the better, and you'll move into theirs too, making your life, and the life of your children, richer. You'll stop looking for reasons that you're different from the other families in the playground and start looking for reasons that you're the same. Ultimately, you're all starting your days by yelling 'Get your shoes on!!!!' 15 to 20 times at the top of your voice.

The married mum round the corner with the giant house and three bathrooms might have made you feel inferior and envious in the early days of single parenthood, but once you realise that you have similar interests in politics or music and she always has an open bottle of red that needs sharing, you'll realise that she's just the friend you're looking for. There is no such thing as a perfect family (although the one you're heading is completely wonderful), and get close to any parent, married or single, and you'll realise that they have just as many struggles or worries as you do. Having local parent friends, whether single or cohabiting, is just good sense. They can help with school runs or lift-share for clubs or parties, they can help out in an emergency if you get stuck at work, and often they can remind you why you're not necessarily worse off when they share the details of their relationship with you. You'll help them with school runs, you'll offer to have their kids for playdates and sleepovers, and as much as they are a part of your extended support network, you'll be a part of theirs. Guess what? Being a single parent doesn't stop people from wanting you in their network of parent friends.

How to find them

So we've convinced you that you need a host of different types of friends to get you through single parenthood in one (plus kids) piece. But where do you find them?

Online

Through writing this book, we've actually met or FaceTimed some single-parent friends that we've been friends with online for several years. The lack of previous FaceTime in no way invalidated the friendship as it was, nor did meeting make the friendship more real (although the mutual consumption of wine is always a pleasing side effect of in-person meetings). If you're stuck in the house with your children all day, get online and get socialising. Remember lockdowns? The whole world made socialising an online pursuit. Single parents are just keeping the trend alive for everyone. Over the years we've both had single parents dropping into our DMs looking for a friendly hello and an assurance that everything is going to be OK. Starting a conversation with a stranger online might feel scary but the stakes are so much lower than an in-person meeting. If they don't reply (because, let's face it, single-parent life can get in the way), it's no big deal and you can simply carry on about your day and message one of the other single parents you find on social media or an app. And if they do reply, it might be the start of a wonderful friendship or a connection you can turn to when you're facing a specific problem or celebrating a single-parenting win.

Shop local

Of course, it is nice to have friends that you can meet up and drink coffee with, drink wine with, or do activities that don't involve the ingestion of liquids with too. Finding a local group of single-parent friends can be a pivotal moment on your single-parenting journey. You can go from feeling like the odd one out, an 'other', to one of the gang. Being around other single-parent families makes you realise that the family you're raising your child or children in is not only OK, but it's brilliant. As much as we all want to feel that we can be trailblazers, the truth is that humans, like most species, tend to want to blend in with the crowd. Being around people who are completely different from you is a blessing, it is enriching, interesting and it allows for growth. But we find comfort in familiarity, and in those early days of single parenting when you're feeling lost, familiarity is glorious and it is necessary.

Remember that first day of school, when you didn't know anyone, and it felt like everyone else was with their mates? And that incredible sense of relief when you made your first friend and you just wanted to stick close to them forever because that horrible lost feeling has now passed? The early days of single parenthood can be a bit like those first days of school. Everyone else seems to have their friendship groups nailed down, they're neatly settled into happy family units and you're the new kid, not knowing where you fit in or what life should look like, now. Finding other single parents in your area that you can hang out with will bring you the same relief as that first-day-of-school friend.

How, then, do you find them? You can find local friends on the Frolo Community app by searching for single parents in your area, or attending a local meetup. But if you don't have access to the app, all is not lost. Just remember that around 20 per cent of all families are headed by a single parent, so the odds of coming across one 'in the wild' are relatively high. Chatting to other mums and dads at nursery drop-offs and at the school gates is a great way to find other parents in the same boat as you. Listen to your children talking about their friends, and notice which ones refer to their mates staying 'at their mum's' or 'at their dad's' for example. Once you know who might be a good target friend, text them (class WhatsApp groups for the win here) and ask them for a coffee, or have your child invite their friend over for a playdate; however long single parents have been on their own, once you've been through the process you'll always make time for others going through the same thing and be willing to lend support, comfort and advice. Once you're more comfortable in your life as a single parent you'll feel happy throwing out a group text asking for help with a party pick-up or offering childcare swaps, and you'll find that the other single parents in your child's circles will often be the first to raise their hands to help.

You can also connect with other single parents through dating. Once you're ready to date (for which we'll prepare you in Chapter 13), opting to meet up with other single parents can be a really great way to make connections, whether romantic or platonic. The majority of dates you go on won't lead anywhere romantically, but dating other single parents will not only mean that you have at least one major thing in common (and therefore one topic of conversation minimum) but also that if you get along and sparks don't fly, you'll likely leave with a new single-parent friend in your area that you can continue a friendship with.

As for the non-single-parent friends that will transform your life, think hyper-local. Do any of your children's friends live within walking distance? On the same street or the one behind? If you can get along well with these parents, however little you might think you have in common, you can really build a community that will make life better for you and your children. If you're further away from your family, having a local network of friends and supporters is even more important. Build up your village with other parents who you can rely on for a cuppa in a crisis, help with a childcare emergency or who will grab you Lemsips when you can't get out of bed. These people will make you feel less alone in your loneliest moments, and they won't care that you're a single parent, only that you're their friend. The turning point in these friendships is often the first time you ask for help. Hyper-independence is very common in single parents, but being brave enough to ask the people around you to help can turn an acquaintance into a friend, and as single parents it is often on us to make the first move, as your friends may not want to add to your load by asking something of you. 'Help' is always the bravest thing to say.

My single-parent story

Leon Wenham, solo gay adopter. Leon can be found writing about his experiences as a solo adopter at @lots_andlotsoflove on Instagram

From the age of 18, I thought I wanted to adopt and I also always saw myself as a single adopter or a single parent. Then in February 2018, I was in the photocopier room at work, I picked up the phone, called the number and literally just said, 'I want to adopt; what do I?' I was a true rooky. I had an informal chat, filled out a form, had a face-to-face chat and it just went from there. It was a very intense assessment process, but I'd looked into it for such a long time that it wasn't a biggie for me. They need to know every school, every partner, every employer, every address that you have lived at – it's full-on. Then they speak to your family, to understand your family dynamics. I was approved, and I found my little one less than three weeks later, so it was super quick for me.

My situation wasn't typical. You generally only get to physically meet the child at the point of introductions when you've already been matched with them, after you've been approved to be their parent. But I did a 'bump into' meeting first. I didn't know what I was expecting. I was very nervous, very anxious. I was going to meet him for an hour and felt like: *Right, you've got an hour to decide*. But that wasn't the case. It was funny, because I met him and his foster carer in a soft play, and I've never been inside one, I'm six foot three, I've got a bad back, I'm bending into all these shapes, thinking: *Is this what it's going to be like?!* But he was so funny and cool, and I just thought: *Oh my God, this is gonna be my son!* I was having all these conversations in my head. It was mad (in a good way!).

On the day that I was approved to be his adoptive parent,

I went to the foster carer's home for dinner and it was such an amazing feeling, because obviously I knew then that he was going to be mine, but he didn't know. He opened the door and he remembered me from the FaceTimes and came running up shouting 'Leon!', so then the introduction started: I went up there for maybe five days and then the foster carer came down here for five days. And the rest is history. He's been here ever since.

Being a solo parent can be all-encompassing at times; it can be relentless. There's no plan B, you just have to crack on with it, so that's what I've struggled with. But it's worth it for the happy memories that we've created. It's the little things: seeing him happy and hearing his little cackle. It's just priceless.

9

Moving on Up – Self-Care and Thinking about Moving On

'Find ways to play and take care of yourself as well as everything else you're taking care of in your life. Parent the parent, and that might mean finding sources of support such as a therapist, a community, a group of people you don't necessarily connect with on every level but you find helpful in certain ways.'

Psychotherapist Charlotte Fox Weber

'Tis a very well-known fact that one cannot pour from an empty cup. And yet, single parents up and down the country are trying to do so, right at this second. With so much to do and only one pair of hands to do it all, so many tasks to organise and only one brain to organise them, the risk of becoming overwhelmed is real. When you're running on empty, everything feels harder.

You're juggling so much, there are so many balls in the air; the more tired you become, the more likely a ball is to drop. Looking after yourself is absolutely vital. Picking up and reading this book is an act of self-care in itself – so well done. You are investing in your future happiness, and that is a wonderful thing. Needing (and wanting) to take care of yourself is the opposite of selfish: it's a gift for your children. At the beginning of your single-parent journey, it can feel as if it's taking all your strength just to stay afloat, and happiness can feel out of reach. But putting reliable self-care practices into place at this point is vital, because you need dependable ways to pick yourself up or get you through the tough patches that every parent faces. Throughout this chapter we'll think about how to find self-care that works for you, long-term healthy habits that will make single parenting easier, setting boundaries, and even rediscovering who you are.

If you feel slightly lost since your life stopped following society's script, please know that you are not alone. Becoming a parent is enough to cause an identity crisis in anyone's life. Becoming a single parent is twice as challenging, but there are twice the opportunities too. Later in this chapter we'll talk about how to embrace the opportunities rather than resisting the change.

Self-care and coping

First up, we need to talk about self-care. And by self-care, we don't just mean bubble baths (lovely as they are). Finding a self-care routine is a key part of being a grown-up, but it stops being optional when you are responsible for kids as well as yourself. If you don't care for yourself, you will categorically not be able to care for your children – it is as simple as that. In Chapter 1 (Making The List) we asked you to think about some self-care, including naming three things that you can do to feel a bit better when you're feeling low. Having a minimum of three go-to activities or practices that can lift your mood or calm you down is important, and they should be incorporated into your life regularly, not just when you're at a crisis point. The idea is that a careful and thoughtful self-care regime will prevent you reaching a crisis point in the first place. You should also have at least one person (and preferably several) you can call on when you need support.

Being a single parent can be a recipe for hyper-independence (that is, refusing to rely on anyone else and being completely self-sufficient, leading to emotional avoidance), which can feel safe when you have a lot of solo responsibility. Unfortunately, hyper-independence can be related to a past trauma, so if your first instinct in a crisis situation is to shut yourself away and stew, there is probably a good reason why your nervous system is telling you to do so. This is one of the times we shouldn't listen to our gut, though. Having people who you can turn to in tough times is absolutely vital. In the last chapter we spoke about the importance of having other single parents to talk to about what you're going through. Once you land in the right chat thread, WhatsApp group or Frolo forum you'll feel a weight immediately lift. Someone will have gone through exactly what you're going through right now, and they will be able to empathise and offer advice.

Aside from your single-parent crew, having a friend or family member who knows you inside out and always has your back is invaluable. If you can, have people you can rely on to fulfil different needs. Maybe you have an aunt who you can just sit in silence with while she puts the kettle on for you, and an instant calm descends over your body. Maybe your next-door neighbour can fix the fence if it falls down or take packages in when you're at work. Perhaps one of the school parents can be your fall-back to pick up your child if you get stuck on a broken-down train and won't be back for pick-up. These people will slowly but surely become the support network you need to thrive as a single parent, and don't forget, you're a part of theirs too. That same school parent can call on you when they have a work trip and need you to do a drop-off for them. Just don't take on more than you're able to, and definitely make sure you have equal (or more) people on your list as have you on theirs. Solo parents can get a bit of a (totally valid) reputation for being super-heroes, and everyone wants their local Wonderwoman or Superman to be on their emergency call list.

What makes you feel better?

Right, let's iron out the details of these, shall we? First, to those self-care activities we've asked you to pin down. Grab your pen and write down three things that always make you feel better. Hold on, we have a few rules. Only one of them can be an 'unhealthy' activity. Your three activities that make you feel good can't be 'smoking, drinking and eating peanut butter out the jar with a spoon'. If possible, all three of your self-care activities should be things that will not only make you happy, but will also have an overall positive effect on your mood, your lifestyle or your body. Try to choose things that are not just distractions from pain but steps to actually heal it. There are no hard or fast rules as to what they should be, but it's useful to know that there has been research into effective ways to break a stress cycle. In their book *Burnout: The Secret to Unlocking the Stress Cycle*, Amelia and Emily Nagoski identify a number of ways to 'complete' the body's stress cycle, including deep breathing, physical activity, creativity, crying, laughing and physical affection. For some of these, you'll obviously need the second element we've spoken about: people to depend on. Who can make you laugh, even when you feel completely hopeless? Whose hug makes everything better? (The little ones are quite good for this one.)

There are others you can have in your arsenal for independent self-care at any time. Physical activity is a great one, and it doesn't mean that you have to pump iron at the gym every day or pound the pavements whenever you feel low, but movement is a great way to get out of your head and into your body. It's even better if you can get out into nature: a walk in the woods – deep breathing and holding your child's hand will tick three of those methods in one go. There you go: single-parent multitasking at its best. With this information in mind, pause and write down all the possible self-care activities that could form part of your wellbeing routine. Other suggestions include journaling, meditation, running, reading, listening to a podcast, having a cup of tea, yoga, gardening, bubble baths (yes, hack, but they are pretty great), knitting, colouring, crosswords, or a phone call with a friend.

Be realistic about the time you have for your self-care activities, but make them a priority. James Hunt has very little free time, as he is a co-parent of two autistic sons, as we have seen, and has one of them living with him at any given time. But he stresses the importance of not trying to pour from an empty cup. 'I used to have more support with the boys, because my parents were able to help out, but that's not possible now, things have changed. But it's just making the most of whatever time we have, it doesn't have to be a whole weekend free. For me, whatever time the boys go to bed, I have an hour to myself. Unless I'm exhausted and I pass out, I'm going to read a book, watch a box set. I will do something. When the boys are at school, I will figure out a way so that I can go to the gym, or I can go and meet someone for a coffee, even if it's for half an hour.

'Whether you're a single parent or not, when you've got children with disabilities you feel like you don't have much free time, because they need a lot of support. I really believe

that doing one thing for yourself each day makes a huge difference over time.'

Phone a friend

Speaking of phoning a friend, next let's make that list of
people you'll call in a crisis. Try to identify why they're
on the list and what they're good at. As we've already
mentioned, there's an old saying that relationships tend
to be for a reason, a season or a lifetime. The lifetime
ones will provide the emotional support you need in your
darkest moments because those people know you inside
out. Now's the time to identify the 'reason' for some of
the other people in your life. (If you can't find one, their
'season' may shortly be over.) Making this list might also
throw up some solutions to problems that have been
flagged in earlier chapters (such as childcare or financial
support from a source you hadn't thought about), or it
may illuminate some areas in which you need to bulk out
your contacts.

　　Never underestimate how brave it is to ask for help
when you need it. And don't forget that it feels good to be
needed too: the people you ask will feel glad you did.

Boundaries for self-care

Good self-care practices are inextricably linked to setting
good boundaries. Boundaries (we told you we'd bring them
up a lot) are most frequently talked about in the context of
romantic relationships, but we need to set boundaries with
ourselves too (and our kids). If you're not familiar with the

concept of boundaries, a basic explanation is about figuring out exactly who you are, and what you need, and drawing a line around that. That doesn't mean that you can't do things for others, or make compromises or sacrifices, but nothing you do should cross these 'boundaries' that you've set for yourself. Nothing we take on or give out should be at the expense of ourselves, or our own mental or physical wellbeing.

When you're in an abusive or dysfunctional relationship, these boundaries are often completely non-existent, in that you are existing only to fulfil the needs of another, and ignoring your own identity and needs. Sound familiar? Welcome to parenting! It is our job to make sure that our relationships with our kids are healthy, and we therefore have a responsibility to model healthy boundaries to them, too. Our needs are just as important as theirs. We're not here to tell you what these boundaries ought to be, we know that single and solo parenting throws up all sorts of unique situations that bend boundaries and break rules, but being aware of what lines shouldn't be crossed is really important, not just for you, but for your kids too; for example, as soon as your child is old enough, perhaps you should establish a rule that when the bathroom door is closed that means the person inside needs privacy. It might sound obvious, but single-parent households often lean towards the slightly less ordered (or is that just us?). Likewise, having physical spaces that are just for you will give you mental space when you need it too. Perhaps you could make your bedroom a private place that your kids need special permission to come into? In turn, they can set a boundary that their room is their private space where you have to ask them before entering.

Modelling this sort of practice helps maintain both yours and your child's sense of independence, as well as re-establishing the parent–child model that gives your child the safety they need rather than the in-this-together team that gives children too much responsibility. Single parents often fall into the habit of asking their children's opinions on decisions that would traditionally be kept among the adults (such as, 'What shall we have for dinner?' or 'Where do you fancy going this weekend?'), which might feel like a nice way to include them, but it could be giving them too much responsibility. This might be a boundary that you need to set in place for yourself: to make as many decisions on your own (or with the help of another adult that you call on when you need help) as you can, and save only the occasional fun ones for the kids to pitch in on (for example, 'sweet or salty popcorn for movie night?').

Boundaries will also extend to other areas of your life and almost always improve things. Stopping replying to work emails outside working hours equals setting boundaries. Waiting to reply to your co-parent's message until after you've had time to think equals setting boundaries. Only allowing yourself a 10-minute social media scroll rather than wasting two hours a night of zombie-scrolling when you could be sleeping equals setting boundaries. Once you realise how positive applying boundaries can be to your life, you'll be getting stricter with yourself in multiple areas and reaping the rewards. Who said parenting was just for the kids?

Healthy habits

We've spoken about getting into good mental-health habits, so here's a quick note on the importance of healthy habits in other areas too. When you're going through a period of stress, it can be tempting to turn to unhealthy habits to cope. Comfort eating, junk food, takeaways, drinking ... we all have our vices and go-tos during hard times. But now that you're moving out of the initial baptism of fire that is new single-parent life and into the never-ending high-speed roller-coaster that is mid-to-long-term single parenthood, it's time to think about establishing healthy habits for both you and your kids.

It's important to establish healthy money habits too. This means meal prepping whenever you can rather than take-aways or ready meals. If money is tight, remember to focus on nutrition over quantity – wasting money on nutritionally empty snacks such as crisps or biscuits kills time rather than hunger when they're asking for food. Nuts, fruit and veg make better snacks (frozen fruit has a longer shelf life and is a delicious treat) and nutritionally dense breakfasts such as eggs or overnight oats can be just as affordable as sugary cereals or toast and will keep them fuller for longer, as well as offering them more nutritional benefits. Put as much care and thought into your diet as you do your kids', and remember that by keeping yourself healthy, you're looking after your children too. Are you eating leftovers off your kids' plates over the sink before scoffing a protein bar while running a bath? You deserve better. The same goes for keeping active, if you can walk the school run, avoid jumping in the car. Go to the park after nursery or get everyone out on their bikes at the weekend. You're boosting your mood, and that of the kids, and you're setting them up for a healthier lifestyle in the future too.

With all this said, when you need to rest, rest. When you need a glass of wine or a takeaway, have one. Everything in moderation, the good and the bad, but try to make the healthy bits outweigh the treats, if you can. This can sometimes be a challenge for co-parents that get into a cycle of competition with their ex, particularly if your child (allegedly) gets more

treats or unhealthy snacks at their other home. This is where
boundaries come into play again: your home, your rules.
Being able to depend on your consistency will make them
feel safe. Not to mention healthier, with all the superfoods
on offer at dinnertime.

Sleep

Glorious, wondrous, precious sleep. Every parent knows
what a lack of sleep can do to our health and wellbeing, both
mental and physical. If you're struggling to sleep, it can feel
as if you're going slowly mad. Prioritising good sleep health
is absolutely vital as a single parent, whatever your situation.
Think about how much thought and time we put into creating
good sleep habits for our children right from the moment they
are born, but how many of us do the same for ourselves? It
can feel really tempting after a long day of solo parenting or
working all day before doing dinner, bath and bedtime, to
capitalise on some child-free time and settle down for a solo
dinner, get online or zone out in front of the television. And
if you have time to do this and get a good night's sleep in,
that's great, but if you're low on energy, prioritising getting
a good night's sleep over a sliver of me-time might be the
better choice.

Likewise, if you have a night off, it can be appealing to get
out, let your hair down and drink 15 Jägerbombs with your
friends, but if you're regularly prioritising this over sleep, you
will likely struggle to replenish your energy levels and feel at
your best. Establishing good sleep health for yourself, at any
age or stage, is always a great idea. Try things like turning
off digital devices before heading to bed (you can set up your
phone so that emergency contacts can still reach you if you

need to on nights you're not with the kids). Keep a regular bedtime and rising time as much as possible. Try not to eat too late at night, and cut down on caffeine and alcohol.

Learn to say no, or cancel plans (with as much notice as you can, of course) when you need to prioritise sleep. Everything will look better in the morning, and you'll be able to tackle the next challenge just that little bit more effectively if you've had a solid eight hours.

Moving on

Once your self-care regime is in place, your healthy habits are established, and you're setting boundaries left, right and centre, single-parent life might be starting to move past the 'survival' stage and into the elusive 'thriving' phase: when things start getting a little bit easier, and you start feeling a little bit less as if you're trying to tread water in an icy lake wearing a pair of Doc Martins and a bomber jacket, and slightly more as if you're a swan, gliding down a river on a crisp autumn morning. Of course, under the surface there's still a fair amount of thrashing going on (single-parent swan-style), but the bits on show are going swimmingly. It is at this stage that you might be thinking about moving on.

When we say moving on, we do not mean dating. For the people at the back, one last time: single parents do *not* need a partner to be a complete family. 'Moving on' will look different for everyone. By moving on, we mean moving out of the adjustment period of newly single-parent life, and into planning for the future. We mean having the headspace for things that aren't just day-to-day survival. We mean reaching the end of the mammoth mega list we forced you to make in Chapter 1 and finally having the headspace to have some fun.

Moving on might mean applying for a new job. It might mean planning your first night out with your single-parent friends. It might mean thinking about a holiday, or starting some renovations on your house. It might mean moving to a new place, or reconnecting with an old friend. Hell, we know we said it wouldn't mean dating, but maybe it might mean going on a date. It's about being open to new beginnings, settling into single-parent life and realising that it has all the excitement, wonder and opportunity of any other life. In fact, it has more, because you already have one or more beautiful little humans by your side to experience it with.

Retrain your brain

If being a single or solo parent feels as if it is holding you back from any of those things, or will be a barrier, please don't worry. As we already covered in Chapter 7, single parents have been given such a bad rep over time it takes a lot of unlearning to believe that life as a single or solo parent can be a truly positive experience. One great piece of news is that we have total control over our own thoughts and beliefs, so if we choose to think that single-parent life is the best possible way we could be living right now, we get to believe it. Everything you believed before (perhaps some negative thoughts about single parents or their limitations) was also optional – it doesn't make it truer just because that thought came first. To give yourself the best possible chance of turning the tide, there are some really important habits that you should get into – we'll tag these on to your self-care regime if you're finding it harder to reach the point of being moving-on-ready. Firstly, that thing we just told you about us getting to choose our own thoughts: it's important. Remember it whenever you find yourself thinking something negative, and try to correct your wayward brain. If your toddler is having a meltdown in the middle of the supermarket and your first thought is: *This would be so much easier if I had a partner to help me deal with this,* try to reframe with: *I am the only person who has the knowledge and strength to deal with this situation right now.* One diminishes your position; the other empowers it. If you can't do this in the moment, try to apply these thoughts retroactively. Post-meltdown remind yourself: *I thought I wasn't strong enough to cope with that alone, but I proved to myself yet again that I can do this all by myself.*

Remember to catch yourself feeding into negative stereotypes or beliefs with confirmation bias too. If you have a pre-existing belief that single parenting is tough, overwhelming or never-ending, you might find yourself logging every time you experience one of these feelings and further enforcing that view, thereby making thriving as a solo parent even harder. If you choose to actively see single parenting as an opportunity, a gift, a joy or a privilege, you can start to note these feelings in the moment as your core parenting experiences and feed into your feeling of coping or thriving as a solo parent, instead.

The next time someone compliments your child's behaviour or one of their talents or manners, remind yourself of how much you do for them on your own, and allow yourself to congratulate yourself too. When your child wakes up in the middle of the night crying from a bad dream and needs comfort, remind yourself that you're the only person in the world who can share this precious moment with them, and that these moments are fleeting. (If you're reading this with a baby that wakes constantly, please disregard that one, we're referring to rare night wakes in older children – we can't paint the no-sleep early portion of parenting as precious with any mind magic; it is hell.) Focus on experiences gained, not opportunities lost. Think of all the ways you have grown as a result of becoming a single parent, whether it was through choice or thrust upon you.

Be playful

Single parenting can feel like all work and no play sometimes. But you know what all work and no play makes you? That's right: Jack – a dull boy. It's important that as well as caring for our children, we care for our inner child too. Psychotherapist Charlotte Fox Weber says: 'In vulnerable moments, it's easy to forget that you're an adult. You might have a terrified inner child, but you're also a capable grown-up. That said, no one feels entirely grown up, and responsibility is unbearable for everyone. Take care of your inner child by insisting on having fun wherever possible, however you can. Playing is one of life's miracles, and it's something we all need to cultivate and nurture throughout life. If you don't insist on playing, it won't happen. Insist on it, no matter how serious life feels, and no matter how scarce. You can play conversationally. You can play by listening to music and dancing badly. You can play by experimenting in the kitchen, making the occasional mess, behaving mischievously with a friend.'

Ask for help

Don't be afraid to ask for help in overcoming the circumstances that led to you becoming a single parent if they are providing you with a barrier that's stopping you from being able to move forward. Grief, trauma, depression and anxiety can all make the tough job of single parenting harder, or even impossible. Reframing your circumstances, as we've asked you to do here, will not be possible for these things. Asking for help when we need it is vital, not only for ourselves, but for the sake of our children. We deserve to be happy, and our kids deserve happy parents too. If you need help, and you're not sure where to start, get in touch with Gingerbread, the single-parent charity, your local GP, or one of the people on your support list we made earlier in this chapter. The most important thing is not to cut yourself off. No single parent should be an island alone. You're part of an epic archipelago, now.

My single-parent story

Holly Matthews, widow and single mother of two. Holly is a life coach and author of The Happy Me Project

I was an actress for a long time. I started when I was very young, just 11. I grew up with all of that and I always thought that would be my world. Then I became a mum when I was 26. I was juggling, as was my husband – we were both very entrepreneurial people. My husband was diagnosed with brain cancer in 2014. My two daughters were just one and two at the time, they were just babies. We just had to get on with it. For three and a half years, Ross had brain cancer. And we went through all of the rounds of surgeries, chemo, all the stuff that goes with it. Our roles shifted, and I knew that there was an inevitability that, at some point, I'd be doing it on my own. I had that at the back of my mind, even if I didn't really want to fully allow that space. But both Ross and I are very direct in our approach to life: Ross had autism and I've got ADHD, our directness runs through it, we just got on with stuff. We had the uncomfortable conversations about when Ross would die. Believe me, they were not nice conversations. But I also knew that if I didn't have them, there would be words left unsaid.

Ross died in 2017 of brain cancer. And before that I was already beginning to be a single parent. The girls were four and six, but in their early years Ross and I were in the house all the time. We'd pick them up from school together, so he was always there. And then he wasn't. And that was really jarring for the girls. I've always been independent, so that never scared me. But I don't think the reality of being a single parent can hit you until you're a single parent all the time.

The day after Ross's funeral, I took the kids to Butlin's on my own. Everyone around me freaked out because they were like, 'She's not going to be able to cope on her own.' And I was like, 'I'll be fine. I might cry, I might find it difficult, but I'll be fine.' And that's kind of how we've been since Ross's death.

Holly's advice

Listen to yourself. Turn down the noise of how everybody else thinks it should be for you. There's an awful lot of opinions when you go through something like this, and people put on you what they think they would do in your situation. A lot of that is pure fear, looking from the outside in. What I did in going it alone might be completely alien to somebody else: they might want to be wrapped up by other people and need help and support. And that's perfectly valid, if it feels right to you. Sit with yourself for a minute and think: *What do I need?* And don't judge what that is. You get to decide. Protect your space and be really honest with what you need.

And any other single parent you see: just high five them!

10

Take Time Out –
You Know You Need It

'At first I would drink and cry and just felt
overwhelmingly that it's not natural for a mother to be
without her children. But now I make the most of it.'

Co-parent Bethie Hungerford

It's time to start moving on. That doesn't mean one thing in
particular, but one universal 'first' for every single parent is
that elusive first night off from single parenting. A night off
from parenting? Brilliant! A night off from parenting, alone,
without them sleeping soundly in the next room? Terrifying.
Whatever you're feeling about spending a few hours, an entire
evening or a whole night away from your kids, it is completely
normal. If you feel all the feelings (excitement, guilt, stress,
exhaustion, fear), that's normal too. The only thing scarier
than being with your kids all day, every day, is not being with
your kids all day, every day. If you're a solo parent with no co-
parent or regular childcare, your first night off, or even break
of a few hours, from lone parenting will likely be precision
planned. Someone might have coerced you into taking one,
saying you needed a night off (spoiler: they were right).

If you have shared custody of your kids, however, it's likely that your first nights off from single parenting will not have been through choice. When your children are with your co-parent, you might feel completely lost. Feeling low when your children are away is completely understandable, as is wandering into their room, curling up on their bed and cuddling their soft toys while watching *In the Night Garden*. Wallowing in the sadness, although undeniably appealing, isn't all that constructive, however. It's much better to actually make use of the time to rest and recharge. We've already spoken about trying to pour from an empty cup; well, a night off from the kids is your chance to refill that cup, baby. But what do you fill it with? 'Sleep!' we hear you cry. It's certainly one option. Going to bed early and sleeping until past 8am is a perfectly valid use of your night off. But how about other things that might be missing from your single-parent life. Adult conversation? How about a night at the pub with friends? Or having mates over for pizza and drinks and conversation that can get as loud as you like? Maybe single-parent life has been low on dancing? It's time to go raving. Remember sex? You could spend a child-free night or two doing that too. Whether you are a co-parent who has to take time off from your kids, or you're a full-time lone parent, having nights that are only about fulfilling your needs is vital.

Parental guilt

We'll let you into a secret right now: non-single parents (cohabiting, 2.4 kids types) also need nights off from their children, they just don't seem to take them. Every seasoned co-parenting single parent has been told by married friends time and time again: 'What I wouldn't give for a night off like the ones you get.' As we covered in Chapter 7, cohabiting parents

seem to fail to understand that they can leave the house literally at any time they like, if the other parent is there. When
this is pointed out to them, however, they usually reply with,
'Oh, I couldn't possibly, I'd feel so guilty being away from
them.' Although they are probably being sincere, this is actually an incredibly thoughtless thing to say to a single parent
who shares custody of their kids. The undertone is that 'being
away from your kids' should equal 'feeling guilty'.

We've already talked a little about how common feelings
of guilt are among single-parent families, for not fitting the
bill of what society paints as the 'ideal' set-up. We also spoke
about how there can be some competition or divides among
the single-parent community of what constitutes the title of
'single parent'. Those who share custody with an ex-partner
are not only carrying guilt at not fitting into society's family
structure, but now they also face further guilt at not being the
sole or primary carer for their child. Some co-parents choose
to split their child's time equally between two households,
because that is what they believe is best for their child. Does
that mean that they don't miss their child like their actual
heart has been taken out of their body and sent to another
place where they can no longer feel it beating but they have
to continue functioning, regardless? It does not. Others categorically did not want to have a 50/50 custody split, but the
decision was taken out of their hands. To add a burden of
guilt to these people that they somehow don't qualify as a
single parent because even though they parent alone 100 per
cent of the time when they have their children, they have to
face 50 per cent of their time alone, without their kids too, so
they're somehow unworthy? We say not.

Single-parent guilt is insidious. It creeps into every portion of your life. When you're at work you feel guilty for not
being with the kids. When you can't make the work drinks

because you have to be home with your child, you feel guilty. When you resent having to pass up a night out because you don't have childcare, you feel guilty for feeling resentful. We're so used to seeing our single parent set-ups, whatever form they take, as 'less than' that we carry doubt (and with it the potential for guilt) over every element of our family lives. You cannot afford to feel guilty about needing a break. Those cohabiting parents that 'would feel too guilty' to take a break – they can choose to take one, they can choose not to. There is someone else there with them to share the load or to pick up the pieces if they burn out. We do not have that privilege, so if you're a co-parent and you have enforced nights off in your schedule, make the most of them, guilt-free. If you're a lone parent and you have your kids night after night after night, find some childcare and make some time and space for yourself. We are all single parents. We all need a break.

Making plans

So we've settled that once and for all: we all need a night (or at least a few hours) off. But what to do with it? The great part is that this is entirely and completely up to you. Perhaps you'll want to use your night off to go on a date? (Wait until you've read our dating chapters 12 and 13 before you embark on this!) Maybe you'll use your night off to get eight hours of glorious, uninterrupted sleep. Or perhaps you'll find ways to make yourself feel like yourself again, away from just being mum or dad.

Co-parent Bethie Hungerford, @hungermama on Instagram and author of *The Hungerpots Cookbook*, found being away from her children incredibly painful at first. But she's learnt to use her nights off to rest and recharge. 'I am running my own business; I work while they're gone. I go on very few dates; my time is precious. If I can lie in bed listening to a podcast with a glass of wine, I would rather do that than be on a date with a stranger. I recover and recuperate.'

Natalie Alexis Lee (@stylemesunday) agrees: 'I'm a bit of a hermit these days; I literally have a bath and listen to a podcast or watch TV. I potter around the house. I really love my home.'

On the other hand, a single-parent get-together fuelled with drinks, music, dancing and group lamenting is always a good idea, too.

Ten ideas for child-free time

We asked the Frolo Community what their favourite thing to do with their child-free time was. Here are some of our favourites:

1. Go for a long run.
2. Go to an art gallery or a live music event.
3. A walk on the beach, with no moaning from the children.
4. Have lunch or a cuppa with a friend.
5. Have a quick nervous breakdown!
6. Go out drinking cocktails into the early hours.
7. Sleep in past 5am.
8. Eat junk food and watch TV.
9. Have lots of sex.
10. Lie down, for as long as possible.

11

We've Gotta Get Out of Here – Holidays with the Kids You Can Actually Enjoy

Hooray, we're all going on a summer holiday! Except that there is only one adult, the hotel still wants to charge the same as a family of four, there's nobody to help with the bags, and one child is trying to open the emergency exit door while the other is trying to shove a raisin up the nose of the person next to them. Holidaying with kids as a single parent, on paper, isn't all that relaxing. It is the kind of work that you might need a holiday to recover from; however, if you swap out the word 'holiday' for 'adventure', the whole experience becomes a lot more appealing (and realistically named). Family holidays should not be reserved for the traditional mum, dad, kids set-ups. And they should not be reserved for those on two-person household incomes, either. You deserve to make memories as your twosome, threesome, foursome or more-some, non-traditional family set-up, and we promise you that it's not only possible, but single-parent holidays can also be the stuff of (admittedly quite active) dreams.

Who is it for?

Before having kids, you might have looked at parents paying thousands to take their two-year-old to Disneyland and thought: *They won't even remember it! Madness!* We're not saying that you're wrong, but you will also know that the minute you have kids, joy stops being solely derived from your own pursuits but starts being about seeing your child experience joy too. That two-year-old might not remember meeting Buzz Lightyear in a year's time, but the parents (with the help of a smartphone) will have that memory locked down for life. This mindset is very much needed for single-parent escapes. Travelling with kids as a solo parent is not relaxing, but it *is* a pursuit of joy – it's just that the joy will likely be second-hand. A single-parent holiday with kids, young kids in particular, is about adventuring with your children and seeing the world through their innocent, open-to-wonder eyes. Keep this in mind when choosing your destination and setting your budget. Single-parent holidays with kids do not need to be luxurious, particularly if luxury is not realistic in your budget.

Think about your fondest memories of travel from your own childhood. They probably involved playing outdoors, building sandcastles, jumping in a pool (any pool), eating ice creams, laughing with your family or friends. Campfires, marshmallows, suncream, pastries, postcards, boiled sweets. On the other hand, marble bathrooms, coffee machines, pillow-soft-beds: these are things of adult vacation dreams, and, let's be honest, the kids will get in the way of enjoying them anyway. Keep things simple and focus on what's fun over what's fancy.

The great escape

For the first solo getaway, think small. A week on a beach somewhere exotic might sound dreamy, but just as settling into single-parent life is about taking baby steps and ticking off items on one big master plan, solo travelling is best conquered in levels. Of course, there's always one mad single parent that packs their baby in a sling, throws a couple of muslin cloths and a nappy or two in a backpack and hitch-hikes across the globe, posting adventurous shots on social media as they go and making it all look incredibly fun. We must unfollow them. We are not that parent. As we discussed, we are keeping things simple. For the first getaway, how about a day trip? Pack a backpack with snacks, drinks, assorted toys, and get on a train: to the next town, the nearest beach, the neighbouring city. Or perhaps a museum trip, jumping waves on the beach, a football game or a theatre trip to enjoy. If you have never done this as a single parent, it might feel like a lot to take on to be responsible for the entire execution of the day from start to finish, so try to plan everything in advance so that you can minimise stress during the trip. If you are driving, download the directions in case the signal is patchy. Ensure the petrol tank is full and the tyres are pumped. Check your breakdown cover and have the details saved on your phone, just in case. If you're getting the train, pre-book tickets (they're cheaper that way) and have the times written down, setting alarms in your phone so that you don't miss the return, if you need to. Check bus routes and walking routes, and have a couple of options in case any unforeseen circumstances come about. Have some cash (in case you need it for parking or snacks), and make sure you have a water bottle for everyone.

Celebrate the wins

Add a sense of occasion to the day trip so that the children understand what a big deal it is for you all. Single parenting is about celebrating our wins for ourselves and for our kids, and achieving your first solo adventure is a milestone worth shouting about. If you're travelling by car, make a playlist together that you can enjoy on the way and you can go back to to remind you all of the trip. If you're going by train, consider a little treat for the journey: everyone choosing their own magazine at the station before getting on the train is a lovely bonus if you can afford it, and will provide some in-journey entertainment too. Try to pause to take photos along the way if you can, including some videos that will really bring the memories to life. Cram all your heads into group selfies or ask passers-by to take shots for you that you can all be in – so many single parents have phones full of photos of their children but none to prove that they were there, making it all happen on their own. The smiles on those faces pressed against train windows, looking out over the ocean, transfixed on a giant dinosaur in a crowded museum: they're down to you. Capture that second-hand joy in the moments you're experiencing it so that you have it in the bank as a memory for later, when you are having a day of doubting yourself or feeling that it's all too much.

Where will you go for your first day trip out? Pause now and jot down a few ideas. Remember, it doesn't have to cost a lot of money. A day trip on the bus to a neighbouring village or town with a walk along the river and a visit to a new playground or a ramble in the woods to collect leaves and jump in puddles: these are all adventures if you plan them as one. If you can, dream a little bigger and head somewhere new, and find an activity that everyone will enjoy. How about bowling, skating, a show or a live sport?

Once you've conquered the day trip you'll be ready to master the overnight-stay trip.

Overnight escapes

Your first overnighter away from home with your child or children can be a really special moment. Just as with all holidays, getting away from home and leaving the day-to-day struggles behind can give you a real chance to connect with the kids and just focus on being their parent with no interruptions. There's something about arriving at your destination, sitting down after the initial settle-in, and allowing the excitement of your child to wash over you and take you over too. You alone are providing them with this minibreak, you have made it, you are a fully fledged single parent, in action, in the wild, and you are smashing it. You might be in a budget holiday camp, a tent in a field, a seaside B&B or a luxe city hotel – wherever you are, make this minibreak about focusing on yourself and your children. Stay in the room and play board games, make a pillow fort, venture out and discover the local area, get active on the water, see a film, tuck into a breakfast buffet, order room service, toast marshmallows on a campfire. Do something they haven't done before, and make new and exciting memories with your babies. They have everything they need, and you are enough.

Once you've mastered the over-nighter, you'll be ready to plan your first fully fledged holiday. The world is your oyster.

Packing

You are completely capable of having a splendid family holiday as a one-parent family. What you are not capable of doing, however, is sending a partner off to the shops if you forget something vital, or leaving the car running as you run into the petrol station for milk. As with most elements of single parenting, a slightly more forward-thinking and organised approach is best when it comes to travelling with kids. Not that we're obsessed with lists or anything, but making one is really the only way to go, here. Include sections for toiletries, clothes, snacks, drinks, electricals, entertainment and emergency essentials. Emergency essentials should include a basic first-aid kit, some Calpol, plasters, and so on. Don't forget sleepwear, plenty of extra underwear and warm clothes, wherever you're going, plus waterproofs. There's nothing worse than cold, soggy kids being looked after by a cold, soggy parent. (Although a cold, soggy anecdote can add colour to any holiday memory.)

If you have toddler-aged kids or younger, always take the buggy. Airlines will stow it for free, and you will need it for the airport, not just to carry the kids, but as a trolley for your hand-luggage. On holiday it will be a mobile napping station, a sunshade and a queue-aid for tired legs. It is never, ever better to just try to carry everything, even if it feels that you'll have less to worry about.

Take outfit essentials that you can rotate rather than too many daytime clothes; if you're going somewhere hot, the kids will wear swim shorts and top all day every day and you'll wear the same swimwear or shorts too. Evening outfits aren't a necessity if you're planning on early suppers and sleepy evenings and nights bundled in bed together (the best kind). For entertainment, it would be lovely to bring a case full of educational, plastic-free STEM toys and leave devices at home, but this is a holiday, and you want to make this experience a pleasant one. One device plus a charger will not only keep them occupied on long journeys but also keep the peace at restaurants when everyone's feeling a bit tired or the wait time is lengthy. If they haven't played with a toy all year, lugging it to another country probably isn't worthwhile. Bring a favourite book for bedtime stories and a puzzle book or colouring book that you can do together during downtime. Preload your phone or tablet with a few episodes of their favourite show or a family favourite film that you can watch together when everyone needs a little downtime or you're in the air or on a train.

Snacks, snacks and more snacks

If parenting had one tagline it could potentially be 'you can never have too many snacks', and now is a good time to put this one into action. Pack snacks that are compact but are healthy and filling. Nuts, snack bars, wholemeal crackers, dried fruit (small helpings) and veg sticks are all great. Plus, they're much better than sugar-packed biscuits and sweets that won't satisfy your children's hunger but might lead to sugar highs mid-journey, which won't make you the most popular family onboard. Refillable water bottles should be topped up every time you see a drinking-water tap, and don't be afraid to ask cafes and restaurants to fill them for you while out and about, or at least ask them where you can do so. Don't board a train or a flight empty-handed, don't get into the car without a pit stop at the snack shop – nothing kills a moan faster than a full mouth.

Finally, grab a disposable camera or dig out an old digital

camera and let your children document their own holidays. They might shoot a roll full of sandcastle blurs, extreme close-ups of their own noses or meticulously document every ice cream they demolish; either way, they'll have fun along the way, and their snaps will form a part of your magical single-parent memory bank.

Camping

OK, we might have lost a few of you at the title, here. Come back! (And grab your mallet.) Camping has always been, and will always be, one of life's little pleasures. Affordable, accessible to most and full of possibilities, being out in nature is good for our hearts, our minds, our bodies and our souls. And however you feel about camping, kids bloody love it. (This might start to change in the teenage years, but teenagers 'hate' everything until they begrudgingly enjoy it and secretly adore it.)

Aside from being cheap, fun, adventurous and a general good crack, camping is one of the best options for a single-parent getaway, because of the community vibe of campsites. As we mentioned before, single-parent families are sometimes at risk of becoming little islands, hyper-independent and too busy for inter-mingling. Campsites are back-to-basics, all-in-it-together havens, where you are sure to find at least one like-minded person to share a cuppa with and your kids will find at least a few other youngsters to throw a ball about with. The equipment can be expensive, but look out at supermarkets for offers on tents, chairs and all the extras, or ask around at school or in your extended family; someone will have the gear and be willing to lend it to you. If you invest in a decent tent in your early single-parenting years, it will provide you with years of camping opportunities, including spontaneous minibreaks whenever the sun makes an appearance and you have a free weekend stretching ahead of you.

Pick campsites that are near to farm shops or supermarkets for easy access to snacks and treats, and plan fun and free daytime excursions, with ball games in fields, wild swimming in (safe) lakes or rivers, or a beach to build sandcastles and jump waves on. Call the campsite before you book and ask how family friendly it is. Nearly all campsites are child-orientated to some extent. Having child-friendly facilities are not only a bonus (or additions such as an in-camp donkey to pet), but such camps also lead to lots of kids on-site. And that means lots of friend opportunities for the little ones, AKA downtime for the single mum or dad. Introduce yourself to your campsite neighbours when you arrive and get your kids to say hi to all the children too. Pack a couple of extra beers that you can introduce yourself with. Within hours the kids will be forming one big pack of youths: throw a football or a few hula hoops at them and they'll be entertained for hours. Did we say holidays with kids weren't relaxing? Find the right campsite and you might even be able to read (one or two pages of) a book.

Group getaways

A solo single-parent holiday is something of a rite of passage, and once you conquer travelling alone with the kids, you'll feel as if you can take on the world. But once you have gone solo, how about joining forces with a few other groups and making your solo-parent trip a little less of a solo and more of a duet, a trio or a superband? Once you've found your single-parent friendship group (as we spoke about in Chapter 8) why not take them on the road?

Finding single-parent friends that you like and who have kids that your kids click with is the stuff of dreams. Once you've found them, never let them go. Join forces and book an annual group getaway, and make the most of family room-rates, adult conversation, evening cocktails, and enough happy memories to fill a dozen family albums. There are several holiday companies and travel agents that organise group holidays specifically for single parents, both with and without children, which can be a great way to make life-long friends and take the stress out of organising a holiday. These kinds of organised trips do tend to come at a premium, however, and great single-parent holidays don't have to break the bank.

Bigger group getaways tend to come at a lower cost per head, since you're splitting accommodation, food and travel costs between you. You often need less entertainment, as the kids will keep each other occupied, and casual evenings at home with pasta and the local wine are just as appealing as restaurant meals trying to keep the children in their seats. In our experience, single-parent group getaways can be the happiest of times. Although family holidays mean packing up all the stresses of home and taking them on the road, bringing a group of single parents and their kids together means everyone is bringing a fresh, holiday mindset to the party. For a short time, you're not a one-person management team, you're part of a team leadership, splitting jobs, decision-making and childcare duties. This is second-hand joy and first-hand, first-person joy rolled into one.

A quick anecdote from Rebecca: 'When Jack was about four, I teamed up with a group of frolo friends for a camping trip to Dorset. When we arrived at the cliff-top campsite, the field was so foggy we couldn't see the end of our bonnet, let alone any of our friends, but we carried on, setting up camp as we arrived on to the ominous scene one by one. The fog started to lift but in its place came gale-force winds, and after we'd gathered in my tent's porch for a quick evening wine we decided it was time to batten down the hatches and try to get some sleep. Fast-forward to midnight and my friend and her two kids (who had been sleeping at the other end of our tent) were unzipping our door and telling us that it was "time to evacuate", the tent was "going down". I scooped up Jack, slightly panicky, and my friend and I retreated to our respective cars, where I lay on the front seat (of my tiny Fiat) with Jack lying on top of me as if I were a mattress, or some kind of literal mum-doormat (he slept like a log). The next morning, we gingerly gathered as a group and took in the carnage that had been our campsite, made coffee in the back of one of the mum's vans, packed up two days early, spent a glorious day at the beach (which was inexplicably warm, sunny and clear) and then went our separate ways slightly shell-shocked but thoroughly amused. Jack refers to the night we slept in the car as an ultimate holiday adventure. For the following year's frolo group trip we rented a cottage with a hot tub.'

Flying alone

We talk about 'flying solo' a lot in the single-parent world. And the time will come to hop on an aeroplane with the kids and make it literal. Flying with a child or children doesn't have to be as impossible as it might seem. As we covered in day-trip planning, organisation is the key, and this is even truer when it comes to flying. There is a lot to remember when you head to the airport, even when you don't have kids in tow, so the last thing you need is to be pushed for time, arrive without passports, or be filling out visa applications in the baggage queue. Several weeks before you leave, you should have your paperwork in order, apps downloaded, passports ready and lists made up. Start your packing list nice and early so that you can order anything you're missing, and have a separate list for the things you'll want with you on the plane.

Check your airline's advice for flying with kids and their policies on extra luggage. Most airlines allow you to take a car seat and/or a pushchair with you, which they'll take from you either at baggage drop or when you board the plane and stow them for you. We've already covered taking your buggy with you (you'll thank us when they're asleep in it and you're reading by the pool), but what the heck do you do once you're actually on the plane?

Of course, this is a different ball game depending on the age of your kids, how many of them there are, and how far you're flying. But the best way to prepare for the plane journey is to think of it like a mini, more pressurised (thankfully shorter) lockdown. Plan in chunks of time and be realistic about how long certain activities will keep them happy for. If you have a baby or a toddler, they might sleep the whole way, but let's be honest, they'll probably bypass that in favour of crying. If you have a flight from hell and your child or children scream the entire way, it will be less terrible if you are prepared for it. (Pack earplugs just in case.) It will also be less terrible if you concentrate on what you and your children need, as opposed to what other people are thinking of you. In your meticulously packed bag will be snacks, drinks, emergency sweets, extra wipes, nappies, milk, all the usual go-tos to prevent or reverse a meltdown. This is not the time to focus on world-class parenting. Forget the STEM toys and the educational books – quiet kids make for fast plane journeys, so think about what they like to do at home to keep them content for the longest. Is it time for the longest Peppa Pig marathon of their life? Maybe a colouring book you can do together would keep them happy? A tricky new Lego set that they'll be able to concentrate on (and tiny pieces you'll be able to scramble under seats to relocate)?

As we've reiterated in almost every chapter to this point, asking for help is OK. Being an island is all right at times, but you're taking your little island on the road, and right now it's crammed into a plane alongside a number of other islands. Getting them onside is the best way to avoid an international conflict, so introduce yourself to your neighbours on the plane, and if someone offers to help you with something, anything, from putting your bags up in the overhead locker to running to grab you some tissues when your baby starts spitting up their milk, please (oh please) say yes. The same goes for the cabin crew; they've seen it all before and will have heard the wall of noise that is a toddler with a pressure headache approaching them in the arms of a frazzled parent many times. They might know a secret trick, have something special they can distract them with, or simply offer to hold them while you go to the loo. Let's end this section with the positive that kids really do often sleep on planes, so make sure you have something comfy for them to lean on, whether it's a big soft scarf or a small pillow, and make the option of a nap as appealing as possible. Alternatively, take a nap yourself and let the kids run wild. There's only so far they can go on a plane.

Car journeys

Never, ever, *ever* set off on a car journey without making sure the kids have gone to the loo. There is nothing quite like driving down a motorway or a winding side street when you're slightly lost or stuck in traffic, with one or more children screaming in the back that they are 'literally going to

die if they don't wee right this second' as your blood pressure
gets higher and higher. When there is another adult in the car
they can calm the child, locate a toilet, aid with finding a safe
place to stop. Your life will be easier, as a lone parent, if your
child has an empty bladder prior to embarking on the journey, and you have a pre-planned road-stop somewhere along
the way. If you're travelling by car you'll have plenty of space
for snacks and drinks (to be consumed in small sips only!) so
don't scrimp on the refreshments.

If you have older kids, make a playlist together that you can
play in the car and sing along to, to make the journey speed by.
Younger riders might enjoy nursery rhymes or baby music (if
you can bear it) or audio books like those by Julia Donaldson,
which they can concentrate on just long enough to fall asleep
for an epic car nap as it ends, so you can continue the journey in
peace, listening to the latest episode of your favourite podcast.
Time your journeys wisely to coincide with napping schedules.
Don't take a long drive just before bedtime unless you'll be able
to smoothly transition your child into bed, or you're prepared
for a late night once they've woken up on arrival. Make sure
you're covered for breakdowns, and if you do have any problems, make sure you tell the roadside assistance over the phone
that you are alone with kids in the car: they will prioritise your
call and get help to you more quickly.

While we're on the subject of car journeys, being able to
drive as a single parent, while not essential, is incredibly freeing. If you live outside a city with a brilliant public-transport
network and can afford a car, or access to one, and you know
how to drive, you'll not only be able to plan road-trips and
holidays on four wheels, but you'll also be able to transport
your children and yourself to safety, in a hurry. How about
adding it to The List?

Now, it's time to scoop up the kids and spread your wings.

My single-parent story

Natalie Alexis Lee, divorced co-parent. Natalie is the author of Feeling Myself *and can be found on Instagram (@stylemesunday)*

I am a lockdown cliché! I told my ex that I wanted to separate during lockdown. For six months we had to live together in the same bed in lockdown. That kind of purgatory is brutal: you're just waiting for your life to start. It took me a very, very long time to actually get the bravery to decide I wanted to become a single parent. I was probably thinking about it on and off for five or six years before I actually did it. Once you've tried everything you've just got to make a decision and do it.

Like most people, finances were probably the biggest block for me. I think I had some self-limiting beliefs that I wouldn't be able to cope on my own, financially. Everything else I was OK with, but I was really worried about taking on a mortgage, paying rent or just being able to feed myself and my kids. That was a huge, scary stumbling block for me. I did seek out legal advice before I made the decision and got some reassurance that I was going to be OK, and what to do in terms of living arrangements. I really wanted to stay in the house that I was in and not disrupt the kids' lives any more than the divorce would anyway, and luckily my ex agreed with that.

I think the first time I actually mowed the lawn on my own was a massive turning point for me: I felt like I was a superhero. I'd never done it before. I didn't know how the lawn mower worked. Despite being a very vocal feminist, I realised how gendered the roles were within our house. That was quite a light-bulb moment. Things like putting up a blind in my daughter's room without asking for help, or putting a doorknob on – it's such a huge sense of accomplishment. I thought my children looked at me with pride, and that felt incredible.

Having full control of the remote, and being able to decorate my house in pink and green, drenched in all the colours that I love, is priceless. It brings me so much happiness that I get full autonomy and control, that's such a lovely, beautiful, freeing feeling. My house is calm, and it's welcoming.

Natalie's advice for new single parents

You probably think that it looks like this big, huge, massive mountain that is impossible to climb. Break it down. Start making lists, start writing the little things that you can tick off and the little things that will take you further on towards your goal. This whole big thing can be broken down into manageable pieces. And slowly but surely you will get there. It's not as scary as you think it's going to be. It's gonna be OK, you're gonna get through it. And there is so much light at the other end of the tunnel.

12

Single and Fabulous – Actively Not Dating and Being Happy Alone

'For me, it wasn't until I was like, "it's actually really okay to be single", that I started making better decisions about men.'

LalalaLetMeExplain, author of Block, Delete, Move On

Single parents are used to hearing 'Don't worry, you'll meet someone else', but you might not want to. And that is perfectly fine. It's more than fine: it's absolutely marvellous. Single-parent life, once you get to grips with it, is pretty glorious, so it's possible that you won't want to give it up. Many former single parents look back at their solo years and describe them as the most magical of their life, so why is everyone in such a rush to give them up? Because we're told we shouldn't love being alone, of course. So many single parents rush into relationships because they're terrified of being on their own, or they don't believe that they can give their children enough if they don't have a partner. But we're not going to do that, are we? Are we?! Not only can focusing on dating before you're ready lead to bad choices and more heartache, but it can also detract from you being able to become the best single parent you can be. If you're working through this book in order (old school – we like it), you'll have already been working on solidifying your status as a financially independent solo parent and making sure you have back-up and support plans in place. These steps should be your priorities, and only once you are comfortable in your single-parent role will you be ready to think about meeting someone else to bring into the mix. And the question we're asking in this chapter is: is that what you really want?

Want or need?

As we've already discussed, single parenting is hard – not only emotionally and physically, but financially, too. Many single parents feel that their only option to feel secure, in all three senses, is to meet someone else and settle down as quickly as possible. But dating out of necessity rather than genuine desire to meet a partner, can be not only ineffective but dangerous. If you believe that the only way to be safe right now is to find a new partner, you're likely to welcome the first person that comes along into your life, without really being sure if they're the right person for yourself or your children. Let's imagine for a second that your pre-single-parent life was on-board (the movie version of) the *Titanic*. Right now, you've been plunged into the water and it feels like you're desperate to be rescued. A floating door comes along. It looks like it could hold you, so you jump on; however, if you had treaded water for a bit longer a luxury lifeboat might have come past and scooped you up, carrying you off towards a better life. And if you'd treaded water just a little longer still, you may have realised you had fins all along and that the water is glorious, here on your own. Regardless, the door was never a good option. Take your time and don't hop onto the first door you see. (Unless you've mutually decided that you're going to get straight back off afterwards and go your separate ways.) Although taking your time, and finding security alone, might feel like the harder option, it will lead you to a happier ending.

We spoke to single mum Layla, a qualified social worker, and dating and relationships educator behind the popular (and brilliant), straight-talking Instagram page @lalalaletme-explain and author of *Block, Delete, Move On*. She says: 'If you're trying to fill some kind of void, it's likely to lead you to date in a way that is not as considered or thoughtful as it might be if you're dating because you are at the point where you want human connection and love, and you're all right with being on your own.'

Based on experiences from her own early days of single parenthood, she recommends asking yourself what you're looking for, and whether you are genuinely lacking love in your life. 'I felt that being loved by a man was the answer to all my problems. And I wasn't paying attention to the fact that, actually, I was getting so much love from this little boy.'

Time to heal

As we spoke about in 'Moving on' on page 195, some circumstances that lead to becoming a single parent are traumatic – quite a few of them, in fact. We're talking adultery. We're talking abuse, both physical and emotional. We're talking divorce, separation and disappointments. We're talking about bereavement and grieving. These are not small bumps in the road. These are road blocks, looming and stubborn, towering over you and blocking out the sun, threatening to crash down on you if you don't make a plan to overcome them and take healing seriously. If the circumstances of becoming a single parent involve any of these, particularly domestic abuse, taking your healing seriously is paramount to finding happiness as a single-parent family.

Steadying your ship as a single parent always takes priority over upgrading to a yacht. Could you be happier in a relationship? Maybe. But you could be unhappier, too. Is that a risk worth taking right now? Slow and steady wins the race when it comes to finding happiness as a single parent, and we've already torn up the rule book with regard to what a happy family consists of, so actively choosing a below-average relationship over yourself just to avoid being alone is completely counter-intuitive. Being intentional about dating, or not dating is the key to making good choices at this time in your life, and until you're healed from the traumas or circumstances that led you here, you won't be clear-minded enough to act in such a way.

The only way out is through

There are many ways to overcome trauma, and to heal from even the most serious heartbreak. Parenting in itself can be healing, as by focusing on the joy of your children you can find purpose in the day to day and give yourself time and space until you're ready to address your demons. Address them you must, at some point. The only way out is through. Getting professional help (from a counsellor, coach or facilitated group therapy) is always a good idea if you can access it. Speak to a relevant charity (Refuge, Women's Aid, Citizens Advice, Gingerbread) who will tell you what your options are, reach out to your doctor, or ask at work if they have access to services that can support your recovery. The self-care plan we set out on page 36 is also vital here. Practices such as meditation, journaling, exercise and time with friends and family are all ways to find peace post-trauma, and once you've recovered, you'll have a set of reliable practices in place for when you have a wobble, or if you fall once more.

Dealing with loss

If you are a single parent following the loss of your partner, the urge to have support to guide you through this time can be enormous, especially if you don't have friends or family nearby to lean on. But leaning into your existing support network, rather than throwing new people into the mix at this vulnerable time, is going to be better for you, and for your children, in the long run. Finding stability as a solo-parent household is paramount right now, and giving yourself the freedom to grieve and heal in your own time, as well as being there fully for your children as they do the same, should be your main priority. (That's not to say that having fun is off the table. Escapism, joy and play are important as you heal, but slotting into something serious right now might not be the right choice.)

Feeling alone

We all feel lonely sometimes, as we discussed in Chapter 7 and elsewhere in the book, whether you're a single parent separated from your child who is with their co-parent and you're home alone on a Friday night because all your married friends are enjoying 'family time', or whether you're on the dance floor at an enormous party, surrounded by people, thinking about the argument you had with your boss earlier that you haven't wanted to burden anyone else with, but that's making you feel completely isolated. The point is, loneliness is a state of mind, rather than a purely physical state. If you're thinking about dating just because you feel lonely, think about whether you genuinely are lacking in connections, or whether there is something internal that you're trying to escape from or need to heal. Layla (@lalalaletmeexplain) says: 'It only feels lonely when you're alone if there is pain in the thoughts that come to your head. It doesn't feel lonely when you're alone if you are well nourished mentally, and you have a great support network around you, and you're feeling loved in other ways.'

If you're feeling lonely and your first impulse is to jump on a dating app, think about what is at the root of these feelings, and whether a romantic partner would eradicate them, or whether there's something deeper that needs addressing.

No repeats

If your journey into single parenthood involved a relationship breakdown or abuse, taking the time to heal properly will also help to prevent you from repeating past mistakes or finding yourself reliving old traumas. If you don't fully understand how you got into a situation, how are you going to prevent yourself from going there again? If you go for a walk and find yourself in a dangerous, scary place, you make a note not to go that way again. Failing to heal before throwing yourself back into the dating world is like putting on your trainers and just heading right back to that stabby alley the very next day (and being surprised when you have an unpleasant encounter there). Unpack what happened in your previous relationships and, rather than focusing on what your partner did or didn't do, think about what you yourself contributed to the situation. This isn't about victim blaming, it's about having autonomy in a situation and taking back control. If you see yourself as passive in your relationships, you have no power to prevent yourself getting into bad situation after bad situation. Until you can make this distinction, you will be much happier remaining on your own, where your autonomy is mandatory.

Fresh start

Of course, some people's single-parent status won't be because of a relationship breakdown or tragedy. Some people came to single parenthood as happy, single people who just wanted to add a child into their lives. For you, cementing that happy, single status with the addition of a child is just as important. Rediscovering yourself as a single parent and learning to love this new, improved version of yourself and your life is key, so take your time with that. Nothing can embed a sense of every-day urgency in your life quite like having a child, but don't let this urgency seep over from the imminent needs of your child's moment-to-moment wellbeing into other areas of your life. Take your time to get to know yourself again as a single parent, because, however you got here, you have a chance at a clean slate. Perhaps you see yourself with a partner again in the future, and this is fine. But taking some time to get to know the new, single-parent you before you start dating is going to have a vastly improved outcome. With life feeling frantic, it can feel as if you're moving at a million miles an hour, but keep in mind that it's OK for different areas of your life to move at different speeds. It's a good idea to keep big life changes separate: changing jobs and moving home at the same time isn't something most people would try to tackle, so becoming a single parent and simultaneously embarking on a new romantic relationship might be a bit much to take on right now. Concentrate on the former, as that one needs to take priority at the moment.

Whether it's the fresh start you chose or not, this is a new beginning. If you were on a train from London to the South of France and your connection at Paris got cancelled, there would be no point in stubbornly sitting on the cancelled train and waiting for it to start up again. You might as well immerse yourself in the city, have adventures and try something new, as scary as it might seem. Your original destination, the sunny South of France, might be coupledom – it's OK if that's still your goal. That's fine, and you'll no doubt get there eventually. But in this (admittedly quite optimistic) metaphor, single parenthood is Paris. You've been handed a fresh start in the city of love. Don't grab the first available stranger you meet to pick up and continue your journey with. Eat a bloody croissant and have some fun.

Choosing yourself

Parenting is one of the most rewarding jobs on the planet. Anyone who has stretched out their arms to a crying child and felt their sobs abate as they snuggle into the chest of the only person on earth who can make them feel instantly better knows that there is no other love like this. Other loves pale in comparison, and it takes something really special to divert your attention. Aside from the rewards, however, are the sacrifices. All parenting involves sacrifices, and single parents get two for one on this front. (Lucky us.) It can feel that day in, day out, the decisions you make and the actions you take are all for someone else. And the fact that you love that little someone more than you ever thought possible doesn't detract from the fact that it can be easy to lose yourself a little in the process. Romantic relationships, while also holding huge potential for reward, also involve sacrifice. They involve generosity, negotiation and hard work. You might be in a place where you're mentally ready and able to invest this in a romantic partner. But you might not. You might, possibly for the first time in your adult life, decide to choose yourself instead, to put that hard work into making yourself happy, to be generous with yourself and devote any time off from single parenting that you do get to making yourself happy. This is not more or less valid than choosing to pursue a partner, but it is a completely viable and valid choice to make, whatever society (or a vocal family member) tells you.

If you're not convinced, let us remind you that there is only one person we get to experience our entire life on earth with: ourselves. Our parents come in and out of our lives, our children are ours for an all-too-short time before they move away to stand on their own. Friends are near and far; relationships are all or nothing. People you've loved with all your heart in the past might be strangers to you now, and the you that you are today would be a stranger to them, too. Rather than giving the precious little that you have left over of yourself from your single-parenting responsibilities to a 'potential future stranger' (not the most optimistic dating bio), give it to yourself. Take time to invest in your own happiness, through play, through discovery, through resting. Choose yourself.

One plus one, not another half

Ever heard someone refer to their partner as their 'other half'? We don't know about you, but we are not interested in half a person as a potential partner. And offering up half a person to prospective new partners isn't much good, either. The single parents from all walks of life that we've met are among the most tenacious, independent, resilient and capable individuals we've ever come across. Thriving as a single parent means standing completely on your own two feet and not only supporting yourself, but at least one other person too. This is a lot to bring to the table in a romantic relationship. People often refer to single parents as having 'baggage', but that baggage is precious, and carrying it has made you strong. The alternative is often bringing nothing to the table at all. You have enough people at your table already, and if someone turns up with an empty plate, you had better send them packing. If someone is looking for you to complete them, you simply do not have the capacity to be that for them right now (and honestly it doesn't sound all that appealing, does it?).

Once you've found your feet as a single parent, you won't *need* anyone else at all, so you'll be dating based on what you *want*, and that will have to add something to your life, not complete it. So many people enter the dating world to find the other half of themselves, the person that will make their life easier in one way or another, and there's nothing wrong with that per se, but being able to stand on your own and thrive is absolutely vital for you, not just now but for the foreseeable future too. Falling madly in love might be your goal, but becoming half a whole isn't an option when you have one or more children depending on you. If you find yourself wishing for a partner to make life easier, or complete your set-up in some way, then you are probably not ready just yet.

If not now, when?

We touched on this earlier a little, but we wanted to circle back to how important it is to take your time with this side of your life. If you've read this chapter and resonated with some of the reasons not to date right now, that's all right. It's more than all right, it's fantastic, because it means that you're facing your situation with honesty and self-compassion. The key thing to remember here is that your parenting and other areas of life don't have to progress at the same speed. Your romantic life and your family life might have matched up neatly before (fall in love, move in together, maybe get married, have a baby, and so on), but for whatever reason, they've now gone out of sync. Many people spend their early single-parent months panicking and trying to get them back aligned. But the truth is, the secret to happy single parenting is realising that they don't have to line up at all. Different elements of your life can run on completely different time scales. It's never too late to land your dream job, go back to school or university, move to another country, or fall head over heels in love with the person of your dreams. It feels as if time is more precious than ever now that you're a single parent, but the idea that time is limited for you to achieve everything else you thought you could or should or would is an illusion. Time feels precious as a single parent, because the truth is that time as a parent, whatever your set-up, *is* precious. Our children grow so quickly. They change, they learn, they amaze us. It feels as if we don't want to miss a second of it, and yet we're so tired and ready for a break. But ask any parent, single or not, how quickly their children's childhoods went. They'll tell you that they passed by in a flash, like sand slipping through their fingers. Bearing witness to their lives, being present for them and showing up unencumbered is the greatest gift we can give to them. We owe them being happy ourselves, and we owe to ourselves to take our time with that happiness.

Once you've fully embraced being happy alone (alone-ish, because moments of true peace as a lone parent are rare), the true beauty in your new single-parent status will become clear. To give it up should take something truly superlative.

My single-parent story

Bethie Hungerford, divorced co-parent. Bethie is the author of The Hungerpots Cookbook, *and can be found on Instagram @hungermama*

The ending of a relationship is hard, regardless, but this felt like 'What the hell am I going to do?' I had been completely reliant on this man since I became an adult and I had a lot to figure out. I had tried to leave previously but didn't have the financial resources or the support to leave. Two years later, I had reached the end of my rope, and I knew I had to leave, so I ended up borrowing money and opening a bank account in my own name without him knowing. I had a friend come with me to see a tiny house that I ended up renting so that when I came back to him a second time I said I'm leaving, here's my moving out date and new address.

There was a woman who lived not far from me and wanted to pick my brain – I didn't even know her name. I went and met her for a coffee and, 10 minutes in, her phone rang and she said, 'I'm so sorry but I have to get this because my friend is just getting out of an awful relationship,' and I just looked at her and said, 'Me too.' She rallied. She said, 'The first thing you need to do is get some accountability – get a group text and tell them your plans.' She made me text while we were sitting there. 'You need money and a lawyer,' she told me, and she made me swear that I would call my parents for money and I would call a lawyer. Once the ball started rolling, I was like, 'I have to.'

I had never paid a bill in my life, so I was terrified, and I had been convinced that I couldn't do it. I had a song that I would listen to that would pump me up, it was 'Light of a Clear Blue Morning', The Wailin' Jennys version. Plus Alicia

Keys 'Girl On Fire'. Oh, and all the Beyoncé! It made me feel empowered. I had no idea what to put on my list; what I needed was the confidence to just do it. And that's how I've approached being a single parent.

I wish I had left earlier – I wish I had just done it. I wish I hadn't got married so young or when I was so naive. I wish I had listened to my family and friends. But I'm learning to forgive the person I was when I made those decisions, because at the time they were the best decisions for me.

I'm happier now than I've ever been in life. My mantra now is, 'I'm doing my best', and that's all I can do. I have it on a hand-painted sign and the kids will repeat it to me, if they can see I'm trying and frustrated. They will tell me, 'Mama, you're doing your best.' And I am.

13

No Baggage Please –
Dating with Kids

Something 'truly spectacular': that's what we've just told you it should take to give up your single-parent status. But where on earth does one find something *truly spectacular* in a world where dating bios contain poetry like: 'no second-hand kids' (trust us: we've seen it)? Firstly, you get ready for rejection (giving and receiving.) Secondly, you buckle up for the ride of your life (metaphorically and potentially literally). Even if you're set on staying single for the time being, you might be thinking about starting a little recreational dating, in which case read on. Even casual dating is different as a single parent, and in this chapter we'll not only run through thinking about what you're looking to get out of dating, but also important topics such as staying safe, protecting your kids, and even thinking about introducing new partners to your children.

What do you want?

You're ready to jump in? Before you proceed, you need to know what you're looking for. They say: don't go to the supermarket hungry, and don't date thirsty – so grab yourself a drink! Take a second, and have a long, hard think about your dating goals before diving in at the deep end. Are you ready to look for a new relationship, or do you just want to go on a few dates and meet some new people to get back into the swing of things? If it's been years since you last dated, you might want to rediscover yourself as a single person or even explore your sexuality. Before Rebecca split from her co-parent she had only ever dated men (well, *man*, singular, actually), but being single gave her the chance to date men *and* women, confirm her bisexuality in her thirties and embark on flings, situationships and relationships with all genders (to varying degrees of success). Success levels would have been higher, or felt higher, however, if there had been more clarity around her dating goals.

A date isn't a failure just because you didn't meet the love of your life. Perhaps you had a great time and a pleasant evening with someone nice. Maybe you endured the most painful hour of your life so far, but you'll have a funny story to tell your mates tomorrow. Maybe you had a night of passion that you can mentally replay to get you through another couple of weeks (or years) of single parenting. If your goal is to be rescued, as we spoke about in the previous chapter, you might be setting yourself up for a fall. But aside from that, any goal you have is achievable, as long as you're being realistic about how to find it, how long it will take, and where you're looking. Are you looking for no-strings-attached fun? That's absolutely fine, as long as you or the people you're seeking it with are aware and happy with the arrangement. Are you looking to meet a new partner? Have a serious think about what qualities you're looking for in that partner, and don't settle for less. Or are you just looking to date and see where it leads? Also totally fine, as long as your expectations aren't set too high (or low) for an open-door, shrug-emoji policy when it comes to dating.

Take a moment now and have a quick think about what you're hoping for when it comes to dating. It's OK if you're fine with multiple outcomes, having fun, something casual, meeting new people, a serious relationship, but write down what you actually want to get out of dating. How you want to feel? What would a great date include? What are you worried about? What are you excited about? Just getting a clearer idea of how you're feeling will help you re-enter the dating arena with a clearer head.

Safety first

There is nothing, and we mean nothing, more important than keeping yourself and your children safe from harm. Being a single parent can feel incredibly stressful for this reason, because the weight of keeping your family safe now falls on your shoulders alone. And opening up your heart, and your trust, to someone new can feel really scary. Here's the thing: it is. There is no way to sugar-coat this part of the story. If you hadn't thought about the safety aspects of dating as a single parent, now is the moment to. In Layla's (@lalalaletmeexplain) experience as a social worker, mums are more at risk than dads in this area. 'There are people who will target single mums, so the less information that you put about your children on your dating profile, the better.

'My advice to single women is just don't invite random men back to your house, get to know them first, go to their house first, go on lots of dates outside in public first. If you have children, you just have to be so much more cautious around these things. Because there are dating safety issues. Since you live in a house with your children, you're a lot more vulnerable. Don't invite people round when your children are sleeping. A lot of mums are tempted to do that. Again, you can do that when you're down the line, when you've trusted this person and you've met their friends. It can be very tempting, especially for those of us who don't have a great support network and don't have a lot of time without our kids to go "Let's have the first date here, the baby's in bed." Just don't do it. That is a safeguarding risk, potentially.'

Keep your children completely separate from your dating life, which means dating outside the house if they are there with their childcare, or even opting to use your nights off to date if this works with a co-parenting schedule. As well as safeguarding for your children, you need to keep yourself safe too. As Layla advises, meeting in public, having daytime dates, having video calls to confirm identity and swapping social-media information can all help to get a clearer picture about who someone is and how comfortable they make you feel. Have safety plans in place and make sure someone always knows where you are when you're dating someone new for the first time.

Take things slowly

Layla says that the other mistake people make is moving things too quickly when they are dating as a single parent. 'Another mistake is introducing them to your children too early. It's different if, for example, you're dating a single dad, and you've got to know each other and it fits to go to the zoo together or whatever. But as a social worker, I saw people moving boyfriends into their homes with their kids, extremely early, like two, three weeks after meeting them on Facebook, these people would be living in the family home. And these are obviously women with a lot of vulnerabilities anyway.'

These cases are obviously an extreme end of the spectrum, but Layla says there is a lesson to be learnt for all. 'I think that there is a temptation to move relationships way too quickly when you're dating with children, because of all the restrictions that you have with childcare, but actually it should be the opposite. You should date ten times more slowly than you do if you don't have kids. And it's a barrier; being a parent is very restrictive.'

Logistics

Being a single parent *can* be restrictive. Finding the time to date when you don't have the kids just won't be viable for all. 'I really do urge people to think logistically: are you able to date?' says Layla. 'Is there any point in even trying to do this? Do you have somebody that can look after the kids once every week? Or once every two weeks? Do you? Can you go out on dates when the kids are at school? Otherwise, is there any point? Because you're going to get talking to someone, and you're going to want to move those boundary lines, because otherwise how are you going to see them?'

Being secure in yourself and sure that you won't be tempted to bend those hard safety boundaries is imperative, so give some thought to whether you truly feel able to make time and space to date at this point. You might remember that in our chapter about work we spoke about doing a sort of audit of your free time available for working and going from there. You can do the same with dating. If you have one night off every week, do you want to spend it dating? Make the space, assign the time, and then choose how you spend it. It might feel that you've taken all the spontaneity and fun out of dating when you have to schedule it so meticulously, but like it or lump it, single parenting is about embracing the joy of organised fun. And organised chaos. Please believe us that if you make the time and space for it, dating can be as fun, wild and chaotic as you like.

Red flags

We've covered pre-date safety, but once you're on the date, how can you spot potentially unsafe situations or dates? 'Red flags' have become a common conversation point when it comes to dating, with people using the term to highlight warning signs for mal-intent or bad behaviours that come further down the line. Being educated on potential warning signs when dating can save you a lot of heartache (or worse) in the future if you take the time to inform yourself; and when it comes to keeping yourself and your children safe that is time well spent. Layla has covered this extensively in her the book *Block, Delete, Move On* and when it comes to spotting a wrong 'un on the dating scene she says: 'If people are asking too many questions about your children, ask yourself, why do they keep asking you? Such as, "Why are you asking for a photo of my son?" Or "Why are you asking where he goes to school?" Or "Why do you keep bringing him up?" If I'm on a date, I actually don't really want to talk about him. Because I'm trying to date as me, not me as a mum. You should follow your gut instinct. If somebody is asking too many questions about your children, and that doesn't feel right for you, take that as a red flag, especially if they don't have children themselves.

'Another red flag would be too much intensity too soon, trying to move things forward too quickly. If they are willing to date a single mum, they have to have patience; they have to consider that you have restrictions in your life. And if they make you feel bad about that, or they try to make you breach your boundaries, or manipulate you, that's a red flag.'

See pages 250–2 for our single-parent dating red and green flags to look out for. Taking these to dinner or drinks and ticking them off like some sort of mad first-date bingo is encouraged.

Setting dating boundaries

This all feels a bit scary doesn't it? So how can you protect yourself out there in the dating Wild West? As we've already covered at numerous other points throughout the book, boundaries are everything: they are there to keep you safe, and they will ensure you get the best out of dating as a single parent. But what should they be? Your dating boundaries should be the things that you will and won't tolerate, both from yourself and others, when it comes to your interactions and meetups with dates and potential dates. We've already covered setting boundaries about how and where you meet people for the first time, and keeping your children well away from any dating situations, but setting boundaries for yourself around interactions with dates is a really good idea too. Perhaps a boundary for you is that you expect a reply from someone you're dating within 24 hours, or 2–3 days. On the other hand, perhaps it's unacceptable to you if someone messages you 23 times a day and expects a reply to each and every one (this is more than fair).

You can set boundaries around ways that it is acceptable for you to be spoken to, the language used, views on certain topics, behaviours you witness or simply gut feelings you take notice of. Having boundaries in your dating life, rather than being constricting, actually gives you a comfort blanket and a personalised guidebook (written and edited as needed, by you) to make things easier. Layla shares one of her boundaries with us: 'When I'm dating, I want that to be the period where I am not a mum. I don't want to be responsible for anyone. If a man says to me, "When are you cooking for me?" Goodbye. I cook 13 nights a fortnight, if you are expecting me to cook anything on the one night that I'm child-free, you can get fucked.'

A- (and we cannot stress this enough) men.

As you navigate the dating world upholding your boundaries, remember that others will be doing the same. If you cross one of theirs, you have to respectfully move on too.

Own your 'baggage'

Having kids is so often referred to as 'baggage' in the context of dating. But in reality, kids are only baggage if you see them that way yourself. (Look at their little faces, how could you?!) Let's be honest, nobody in this world is without some sort of baggage. It's amazing when you're dating at a slightly older age how many people make their entire dating bio 'never married, no kids' as if that means you're the biggest catch on the Internet. Spin your perspective, though, and you might read that as 'Nobody has liked me enough to marry or procreate with me, thus far.' We're not saying that's what it means, we're saying that how you read *anything* is a matter of perspective. If other people see your kids as baggage, that's perfectly fine, but they're not the right person for you; however, if *you* see your kids as baggage that's weighing you down and making dating impossible, you're not ready to date.

In the early days of single parenting, it can feel as if you'd be a more appealing dating prospect if you didn't have a child or children included as part of the long-term package. But as you find your feet as a single parent, banish any internalised stigma and start to thrive in the role, you'll realise that you're even more of a catch as the brilliant, independent single parent that you've become. That won't happen overnight, but it's worth waiting until you reach this point before starting to date seriously to meet a potential future partner, so that you don't end up settling for less than you (and your children) deserve.

In the meantime, however, if you can't shed the 'baggage' weight, fly with carry-on only. Ditch the kids (metaphorically) and date as if you don't have any (in all but the safety arena). Because you don't owe people your entire life. You actually don't owe people anything, apart from honesty and respect. You don't need to tell people that you have children until it affects them. That doesn't mean lying, but if you meet someone out and about and you're mutually interested in embarking on a casual fling, they don't need to know the details of your home life, beyond the fact that you're single. It's OK to actively try and date people who aren't looking for anything serious and that aren't interested in kids so that you can keep your dating and your parenting lives completely separate. In fact, having an active dating life away from the kids is a great way to work on your self-esteem and build a part of your life that isn't just you as a single mum or dad. That doesn't mean not telling people about your children: it just means not owing them information.

Telling dates about your kids is inevitable at some point. And you'll soon figure out how you're most comfortable sharing the news. 'I will drop it very soon into the conversation,' says Layla (@lalalaletmeexplain). 'When I was on dating apps, I wouldn't say it on my profile, but the second they said "What are you up to this weekend?" I'd say, "I've got my son this weekend." You can just drop it in really easily.'

Zombieing, negging and lovebombing

The dating scene has changed, ladies, gentlemen and gentle-people. It's not as simple as meeting someone down the pub or at work any more, and that's that. Dating apps have changed everything. Swiping your way through zillions of options has made many see potential partners as upgradable, disposable, shoppable and probably other -ables that aren't conducive to a lovely dating scene. Realistically, you don't need to know all the linguistics of modern dating, but having your wits about you and sticking to those boundaries we've discussed is your best way to have success when dating.

You've probably heard about ghosting, but if you haven't, it's when someone you're dating just disappears unexpectedly off the face of the earth, almost as if they've died (hence the name). Unfortunately, this happens to almost everyone at some point, and while it's most common when you've just started chatting or been on one or two dates, it can happen after longer situationships or periods of dating too. The only thing you need to know about ghosting is that it is not about you. Trying to find out why you've been ghosted is completely pointless. Blanking someone unexpectedly can have really big emotional consequences, but if you're on the receiving end, remember that it says everything about them and nothing about you. Maybe something bad really did happen in their life. Maybe they met someone they liked more. Maybe they were married with kids the whole time. Or maybe they lost their phone. Not having an answer is painful, but it's not a reflection of you or your worth.

They might come back to life, however! This is called zombieing: when someone comes back from seemingly having vanished, like a zombie from the dead. We do not tolerate zombieing. They'll probably have a great excuse, but you'll likely have heard better ones from your kids about why they haven't done their homework.

Now for the more sinister things to watch for: negging is a term used to describe the act of insulting a date or romantic partner. It is a very fine line between flirty banter and actually trying to break down someone's self-esteem with constant put-downs. They might start off as playful, but beware the overstepping of a mark between playful and just hurtful, or if the insults are one-sided.

On the flipside of the same rather unpleasant coin, lovebombing is something to be cautious of, particularly if you're in the phase we discussed in the previous chapter, of feeling that you need to be rescued. Lovebombing is a tactic often employed by potential abusers or controlling partners, where they shower you with 'love' and affection very early on, but then withdraw this after a period of time, creating anxiety and eagerness to comply with their wishes in order to regain the love (hence the control).

'Watch out for the manipulation of your boundaries and trying to move things too fast,' says Layla. 'Trying to allude to the fact that you're in a relationship very early on: this is lovebombing. That would be the one thing that would worry me the most for single parents: moving way too fast, way too much intensity, way too quickly.'

If something feels too good to be true, it probably is.

Who to date

As we've already said, never date thirsty. Take your time and enjoy the journey of rediscovering yourself through dating, meeting lots of people until you find the right one. (Or until you don't, and decide that dating for fun is all you need at this point in your life; that's fine too.) The perfect partner is going to look completely different for everyone, and you are allowed to decide for yourself what the boxes you're looking to tick are. You might spend the first year of single-parent dating being outraged at people who say that they don't date single parents, before dating a single parent yourself and realising that you aren't willing (or able) to take on more parenting responsibilities, either. This is OK – it is a lesson to learn for yourself.

Having said that, for many, dating other single parents is the perfect choice, because only other single parents really 'get it' when it comes to schedule restrictions, putting the kids first, and having to split your time (and personalities) between romantic you and parent you. For this reason, following from the success of the Frolo app, Zoë launched Frolo Dating, a user-verified dating app where single parents who are ready to date can connect.

Frolo Dating by Zoë

Due to ongoing requests from our community users, three years after the launch of Frolo Community, we launched Frolo Dating as a new mode on the app. We did a lot of research with our users on what the perfect single-parent dating app offering would look like, and here's what topped the wish list:

- A dating app just for single parents (where no one has to see kids being described as baggage!).
- A mindful and respectful dating experience where shared relationship values are taken into account, as opposed to a swipe-right-or-left culture.
- A safe dating experience, where every user is fully user-verified, meaning that they are who they say they are.

Since launching Frolo Dating, we already know of one frolo engagement, and lots of blended frolo families and blossoming romances.

Have fun

Some of this has been quite 'good luck and God bless' hasn't it? But, first and foremost, dating should be fun. Once you're in a good place emotionally and ready to date, and you've worked out what you're looking for, it's time to actually enjoy yourself. Go out to a bar and snog a stranger who you fancy. Get their number and go for a drink with them. Say yes to being set up with a friend of a friend (and then promptly unfriend the person that got it completely wrong). Go speed dating. Tell the person you've always fancied that you have a crush on them. Buy yourself new lingerie or overpriced after-shave, get a haircut, reinvent yourself and learn how to feel sexy again. Fall madly in love with the first person you have great sex with and then realise that you actually just really needed that orgasm and you actually have nothing in common before slowly disentangling yourself over the course of six very messy but exciting months.

Date good people, date bad people, and then realise that everyone is good and bad but the important thing is finding someone with more good than bad that you can bump along with, making each other's lives richer. Date other single parents, fall madly in love and make huge, messy blended families. Get out there and have fun. If fun and enriching your life is your aim, rather than success or failure in the form of a forever relationship being the only options, you are much more likely to win.

Single-parent dating red and green flags

Red flags

- Too much intensity, too soon. If something or someone seems too good to be true, it possibly is. Look out for signs of lovebombing as described earlier.
- If someone is asking too many questions about your child/ren too soon, ask yourself why. Avoid putting your children on dating apps, and be cautious about sharing information about your kids, especially if you're

not chatting to another single parent that you've met on a user-verified app such as Frolo Dating, or in real life. This also includes someone (particularly a non-single-parent) asking to meet your children very early on.

- Someone referring to your kids as baggage, or insinuating that you need to find a partner 'for the sake of your children'.
- App users saying that they don't have socials, keeping you at arm's length, or insisting that meetups take place on their terms, or are pushy about moving things forward. Beware of catfishers (people pretending to be somebody they're not online)!
- Referring to their ex, or worse, all their exes, as a 'psycho' or 'crazy', or telling you that you're 'not like other women/men'.
- Being disrespectful of your time or reluctant to work around your schedule, or repeatedly telling you that they 'wouldn't usually date a single parent'. This subtly shifts the power dynamic in their favour and is a form of negging.
- If you wouldn't feel comfortable introducing them to friends or family, or you find yourself editing what you tell people about them, they're not the one for you.
- If you get a gut feeling that something is wrong or off, or that things feel challenging from the start.

Green flags

- They respect your time, your timeline for dating, and your boundaries. Finding someone who understands the challenges of a single-parenting timetable is non-negotiable, as is someone who understands why you may need to take things slower.

- They see you as more than just a single parent. You might want to keep your parent persona and your dating persona completely apart for quite some time, and a prospective partner should respect that, and want to get to know both on a timeline that suits you. Having said that, if they steer the topic away from your children at all costs and show no interest in your life as a parent, they might not be your forever person.
- If they are a parent themselves, and they light up when talking about their kids and seem to be a great parent to their children, this is obviously also a huge bonus.
- They make you feel that you can be completely yourself around them.
- They are a good communicator, and you're both comfortable talking about how you're feeling and thinking about the future.
- They are working on themselves and open to personal growth, just like you.
- You believe in your heart that they will bring positivity into your life as it is, and that they have potential in the future to bring positivity into your children's.

14

Over the Rainbow –
Thinking About the Future

'My kids are thriving. And so am I. It's the most
beautiful thing I ever did.'

Natalie Alexis Lee (@stylemesunday) on single parenthood

The majority of single parents didn't plan to do it this way, but
you are about to discover your new superpower: adaptability.

Congratulations! You've made it to the end of the book.
Reading an entire book as a single parent is no small task,
so well done – and hopefully you have learnt a thing or two
along the way and are feeling just a little more prepared for
what your beautiful new life has in store for you. Before we
leave you, in this, the final chapter of the book, we want to
talk to you about the glorious unpredictability of single parenthood: how you thought that single parenting would be all
about selflessness, but you actually get to be completely selfish
and enjoy all the beautiful moments with your children to
yourself. You can drink them in and make parenting decisions
that you really believe in, and live a life full of freedom and
love. If you focus on one thing as your goal right now, make
it freedom: freedom from negotiation, freedom from societal
norms, freedom from an ordinary life or taking the path well

trodden. You are free to create a life that works for you and your children, and it can look however you want it to.

Lonely moments are OK

As we've already mentioned, single parenting is, in our opinion, a bit of a misnomer. Technically, if you're romantically unattached, you are single, but you are definitely not alone. Not only are you not alone at home, because you have one or more children to keep you company, talk to you (every single minute of their waking hours, often), and be held by you, but you are not alone because you are a part of the single and solo parent community now, too. That isn't to say that you're not allowed to feel lonely when you've put the kids to bed and you sit down on the sofa and wish there was someone to moan about your day to, or to make you a cup of tea. Or when the children are at their other parent's or at school and the house feels impossibly empty without them. Or when you see nuclear families posting about their cosy Christmases or picturesque beach holidays and you're spending holidays alone or adjusting to a family picture you weren't planning for.

If you feel lonely, allow yourself time to grieve. Actual loss, if you've suffered it, yes, but also to grieve the loss of your life as you thought it would look. We all have an idea of how our lives will look when we're young, and many of the young years of our lives are spent doggedly aiming towards it. If you never reach that picture, or you reach it only to see it slip away, or to be dramatically torn up in front of you, then you will need time to get over the loss. If this experience will teach you anything, it is that life doesn't always look the way you thought it would. And that can be a good thing. Whether now, or when you're ready in a few years, you may be hit with the loss of another life that you thought would be yours. You are allowed to feel sad that it isn't. (Aside: we recently read about the late Princess Margaret's daily routine, where it was revealed that she spent much of her life lounging in bed, luxuriating in long baths, reading newspapers that she left scattered about the floor, drinking vodka cocktails and taking leisurely teas, so if anything, we're grieving *that* as the life we never had.) Grieve that lost life and then grasp your new one with both hands so that you don't miss a second of it. And if you feel lonely, pick up the phone.

Freedom

After grieving the life you thought you'd have, or the one you thought you'd wanted, and coming to terms with your new normal, try to find the positives in your situation and embrace these elements of life fully. Hopefully, we've outlined a few of these throughout the book, but as we mentioned at the beginning of this chapter, the main one is freedom. Actual freedom, yes, in the daily choices you make and the independence that single parenting offers, but mental freedom, too. Once you've let go of the life you thought you were destined for, you will realise that you're free to rewrite your life plan, and it can contain absolutely anything you want. Not only that, but you don't have to stick to the new plan either. There is enormous freedom in making mistakes and surviving hardships, and there is endless capacity for growth. Not only is that freeing for you, but it is also a great lesson for your children.

Beyond endurance

Much of the conversation around single parenting focuses on the hardships of raising children in a one-parent home: the logistics of juggling work and childcare, finances and the home single-handedly. And we're not here to minimise these struggles (which is why we wrote this book to help you navigate them), but we also want you to look beyond the struggles and find the positives in single parenthood too. If you see raising your children alone as a hardship, or something to be endured, you might miss out on recognising and enjoying the positives. There is a serious lack of inspiration when it comes to single-parent success stories, and even less when it comes to single parents being upheld as aspirational figures. Yes, people will say, 'I don't know how you do it' or 'I could never manage it', but very rarely does someone say, 'I wish I was a single parent.' We are here to change the narrative. Single parenting can be something to aspire to, if that life is right for you. It is not selfish, it is not hard on the kids, it is not impossible. There is no one right way to raise kids, except to do it with a heart full of love and a capacity to learn. Single parenting is not simply something to be endured until you can meet someone else or until the children leave home. If it was, we would have called this book 'Surviving Single Parenting' or 'Just Give Up'. But we genuinely are Happy Single Parents. It is a way of life that neither of us would give up unless the alternative being offered was absolutely perfect.

Let your children guide you

As much as you are here to parent your children, remember that they are here to help us learn too. Above all, let your love for them guide you, and you can't go too far off the right path. Treat yourself with the gentle care that you treat them. Maintain your boundaries with them, yes, but be vulnerable with them too. Say sorry when you make a mistake. Let them see you work hard, and celebrate your successes with them. Show them that as well as being there for them, you prioritise your own health and happiness as well. A common thread in our conversations with almost all the single parents that we spoke to for this book, who came to be here by *choosing* to have kids alone and become a solo parent or by leaving a relationship, was that they wished they had done it sooner. Some waited years to take the plunge, for fear of the impact growing up in a single-parent home would have on their children. Each and every one of them told us that their children are thriving. We're not saying it's easy, or that there aren't extra challenges with doing this alone, but children deserve happy parents, and by picking up this book you are actively pursuing that. When you hit a rocky patch and you need a reason to keep putting one foot in front of the other, find it in your children. Take photos of the good times so that you can refer to them in the bad times, when you need a reminder of why you're doing this, and that you're doing it well.

Aaron Dale (@raisingboys_2men) reiterates: 'Being a single [parent], being a [parent] full stop, it's an opportunity. You've planted a seed, right? Under the right conditions, the sun, the water, that seed grows into something beautiful. I have an opportunity to plant that seed, to water that seed to make sure that seed grows. I look at pictures of my children sometimes when they were five and two, and it's just gone so quick. And you think to yourself, why spend all this time arguing over things that are not even going to be relevant in a few years' time when you could just continue to water that seed?'

Remembering that this time is precious is important when it comes to making sure you're spending your energy on the right things. This can be really tough in the hard times, but let your love for your children guide you.

What goes up

A note on those bad times. Single parenting is not a linear path. It is wonderful that you've stuck with us through this book, and hopefully made steps into feeling settled as a single parent, but as with any other area of life, it will be full of ups and downs, and unexpected curve balls. You might think that everything is sorted, only to be hit with something that can throw you off course again; and these things are undeniably tough to deal with alone as the solo head of a family. In these times, try to stay in the present. Just as we walked you through in Chapter 1, Making The List, reaching a far-off point of 'happiness' can feel unachievable in these moments, so keeping things simple and taking it back to the here and now is vital.

When you become a single parent, it can feel as if your whole world has narrowed in, and that the weight of your new responsibilities is too much to bear. In these times, put everything down and pick up only one thing at a time. Imagine your responsibilities are a really heavy load of shopping that you need to get home without a trolley or any transport. Trying to carry everything at once is going to end with a broken back, whereas dividing it into smaller piles will allow you to get the job done. Take things one day at a time, and deal only with the task at hand. Getting the kids dressed for school, making that cup of tea, calling the doctor. Know that this too shall pass and try to be kind to yourself as you navigate challenges. All parenting is a rollercoaster, but the highs and lows of single parenting are just that bit more intense. Embrace the climbs and allow yourself to enjoy the views from the top, and endure the falls or the loop the loops as best you can, with the knowledge that they'll be over soon. You'll get better at spotting the dips as you go along, too, and better at preparing for them. You'll protect yourself against changes in circumstance, brace yourself for co-parenting blow-ups and swerve dating disasters as you become a seasoned single-parent passenger.

Ever evolving

Just as working through the challenges outlined in this book moves us closer to a life rich in contentment, our children's needs change as they grow, and certain situations become easier to manage simply with the passing of time (such as when the kids start school and most of their day-to-day childcare costs vanish, yippee!). As well as being mindful of our children's changing needs, wants and demands, we should be mindful of our own capacity to change and grow, too. Young children may be incredibly full on in terms of their physical needs, but they'll need different things from you as they develop through different stages of their childhood and educational journey. One minute you're rocking them to sleep, the next you're facilitating playdates and practising their reading, then suddenly you're a glorified taxi driver that they need an entirely different (and often non-communicated) type of emotional support from. All different, all challenging, all filled with love (some stages more openly displayed from their side than others). Your life will have to adapt to fit with these stages, but this is not mutually exclusive from the adaptations you may want to make to your own life outside of parenting. Maybe you'll want to change career, find a new partner or move home. These things are possible as a single parent, and you don't have to put your life on hold to be a good (or happy) single parent.

Bear hunt

A quick note on putting your life on hold. A common response to trauma or change is to go into fight, flight or freeze. When faced with the many challenges of single parenting, many are tempted to either freeze (by choosing not to focus on growth in their own life and only focusing on the kids,) or fly (by taking any opportunities to escape, partying too hard on nights off, or making rash life choices). But just like going on that ruddy bear hunt, you can't go over it, or under it – the only way out is through it. The challenges of single parent-hood must be worked through, embraced and overcome. The occasional spot of hiding away from the world or indulging in a bit of escapism is fine, of course, but you might not ever reach the bear (or single-parenting happiness, in this rather loose metaphor) if you indulge in either too often.

Inside out

The truth is, the most important step in being a happy single parent is acceptance. You must accept your situation and choose to feel good about it. Just as much of single-parent stigma is rooted in internalised beliefs; being unhappy as a single parent is often about what is being internalised, too. Not letting go of the life you had, refusing to accept going solo, seeing single parenting as a 'stage' a 'condition' or a hardship. If you are able to truly accept your status as a single parent, and you begin to feel comfortable and confident in your way of life, you will be able to build a life that works for you with no mental barriers to striving for happiness. It isn't quite as simple as 'deciding to be happy', of course, but being open to it and believing – nay, knowing – it is possible is the absolute best start.

What does normal mean anyway?

Raising children in single-parent households has its own set of challenges, as outlined in this book, and depending on what this mad world has in store for you next, there may be a new set of challenges to overcome. So much of family life is still structured around the traditional or 'normal' two-parents-plus-kids narrative that it can be hard to find your feet if you're living life any other way. As you move forward, you might end up in a different variation of a non-conventional family, such as a blended family (where two single parents with children couple up, bringing with them step-siblings for their existing kids). There are whole new sets of things to think about to make a blended family set-up a success (stay tuned for the sequel if we're ever lured out of glorious single parenthood by eligible single parents), and you should draw heart from the fact that you've veered off the path of what's 'normal' before and absolutely smashed it.

Take your time

Not many of the topics we've discussed in this book are quick fixes. They are about laying the foundations of life as a happy single parent. There are no shortcuts, cheats or workarounds. The end goal isn't clearly defined; it isn't a measurable accomplishment or a comparable achievement. It is day-to-day contentment and making the choice to embrace a life filled with love. More important than any one thing we've outlined in this book is making the decision to be patient, and to be kind – with your children, and with yourself. Take your time as you work through the challenges that come your way, and give yourself the room to focus on your children and yourself in all this. Give yourself room to grow, to make mistakes, to do things over, to not do them at all sometimes. Being a happy single parent isn't something you get, it is something you do. You get up and you do it, as often as you can, knowing that it is possible, and knowing that you deserve it.

When we became single parents, we wish we'd had someone to tell us that everything was going to be OK. We are here to tell you: everything *is* going to be OK. When you're lonely, you are not alone, when you are flailing, you are not failing, when you feel guilt, you are not guilty. Your children are lucky to have a strong, thoughtful, curious and kind parent in their lives, and you are lucky to have them in yours. Keep doing what you're doing, because you're getting better every day.

One last thing

The thing we want to leave you with is this. Everything is hard until you get the hang of it: tying shoelaces, riding a bike, learning to read, learning to drive. Let's take learning to read, since you can all do it, having made it this far. When you were learning the basics at school, it felt impossible. The letters were like weird, wavy shapes that you couldn't imagine ever deciphering. You felt frustrated, bored, overwhelmed.

You wanted to quit. But you persevered because you had to. Eventually, you got used to it, and then it became a little easier. Soon you were reading things without noticing that you were even fulfilling the task of reading. It was just happening because you'd learnt how.

Single parenting is just like this. It feels impossible at the beginning. You will want to quit. You'll feel as if you'll never get the hang of it. But you'll keep trying, because you have the single biggest motivator for success on this planet: the happiness of your children. Little by little, the weird, wavy shapes will start to form letters and the day to day will get a little easier. You'll start *doing* single parenting, actually doing it, without noticing that you're working at it. You'll have overcome the hurdles (ticked off everything on The List), passed the learning phase, and you'll be stuck right into the middle of the thing, a successful solo head of a household. A single parent, undeniably doing their single-parent thing.

And this is where the secret ingredient to your life as a *happy* single parent lies. It lies in that very moment when you realise that you are doing your single-parent thing. At this moment you are ready to stop seeing single parenthood as something to be endured, overcome and passed through on a journey somewhere preferable. It is here that you can take stock, and truly judge the weight of your life as a single parent. Not at the beginning, when things are undeniably tough, chaotic and messy, but once you are settled into the rhythm of your new and gloriously independent family life. (After all, you would never ask your child, before they learnt to read, what their favourite book was.)

Some single parents never get to this point. They may reconcile with their co-parent or meet a new partner or form a blended family quickly. They will likely always see their single-parent months or years as something they overcame, or survived. They would have been happy with the aforementioned version of this book titled 'Surviving Single Parenthood'. They may buy into the narrative that single parenting is something to get through and out the other side. But just as the pleasure in reading doesn't come from skimming through the pages to find out the ending of the book, but in getting lost in the story, the joy in your single-parent life comes from being truly immersed and present in the day to day. Notice the way that your child races to you at the end of a school day and leaps into your arms, before you go home and have them all to yourself. Relish the quiet peace in your home after bedtime when you can lay in the bath for hours, or watch an entire series of your favourite TV show uninterrupted. Weigh the cost of your independence frankly, and be honest about the sacrifices you're making (those aforementioned evenings of 'leisure' are often spent working overtime in both our households, if truth be told, and this book was written late into the night, in snatches and stretches of long hours home alone), but don't let the hardships be the whole story. Above all, be open to recognising the beauty in your single-parent life, and be realistic about the alternatives.

Being a single parent to one or more children is hard work, but it can be overwhelmingly wonderful, too. If you look for a moment in each day to prove this, you will find it. Each and every single parent we interviewed for our book is living a life that contains joy. We love single parenthood so much that neither one of us is in any kind of rush to give it up. We opened this book with Kate Winslet's quote about single parenting. She said you carry on 'because you have to'. Finding happiness as a single parent is about finding the space beyond *having* to carry on, and realising that you *want* to. This *is* a life worth aspiring to: we carry on because we *want* to. We choose single parenting.

Now we want you to join us. It's time to get happy.

Resources and Support

Global

Frolo, for finding other single parents near you: frolo.com
App Close, co-parenting communication app: appclose.com

UK

Child Maintenance Service: www.gov.uk/child-maintenance-
service
NHS Advice for single parents: https://www.nhs.uk/conditions/
baby/support-and-services/advice-for-single-parents/
OnlyMums and Dads, for legal support: www.onlymums.org
Family Separation Hub, separation support: www.family
separationsupporthub.org
What About Aruna videos. Videos for separating parents:
naccc.org.uk/free-videos-for-parents-what-about-aruna
Parenting through separation guide: resolution.org.uk/
wp-content/uploads/2021/05/Parenting-through-
separation-guide.pdf
Cafcass Parenting Plan: www.cafcass.gov.uk/grown-ups/
parents-and-carers/divorce-and-separation/
parenting-together/parenting-plan

Citizens Advice: www.citizensadvice.org.uk

Advice Now Guides. Free resources that provide information about all aspects of separating and parenting: www.advicenow.org.uk/topics/family-and-personal

Gingerbread. UK single-parent charity: www.gingerbread .org.uk

One Parent Families Scotland, Scotland single-parent charity: opfs.org.uk

Asian Single Parents Network: aspnetwork.org.uk

Single Parents Wellbeing, Wales: https://www.singleparents wellbeing.com/

Parenting Apart Programme: www.parentingapart programme.co.uk

Single Parent Rights Campaign: www.singleparentrights.org

Working Families. The UK's national charity for working parents and carers: workingfamilies.org.uk

Surrogacy for single dads: brilliantbeginnings.co.uk/ surrogacy-for-single-dads

Widowed and Young: www.widowedandyoung.org.uk

Amicable. For divorcing parents: amicable.io

Refuge. Domestic abuse charity: refuge.org.uk

Ireland

One Family Ireland. Single-parent charity: onefamily.ie

Citizen's Information for Parenting Alone: https://www. citizensinformation.ie/en/birth_family_relationships/ parenting_alone/

US

Temporary Assistance for Needy Families (TANF): www.acf.hhs.gov/ofa/programs/temporary-assistance-needy-families-tanf

Child Care Tax Credit: www.efile.com/child-dependent-care-expenses-credit

Solo Mothers by Choice: www.singlemothersbychoice.org

Jenny Lisk. For widowed parents: jennylisk.com

Single Parent Project. Single-parent charity: www.single-parentproject.org/single-parent-support

HOPE, Inc. Single-parent charity for those on low incomes: hopbe.org

Financial aid resources sheet for single parents: www.gofundme.com/c/blog/financial-help-single-parents

Australia

Australian government child support: www.servicesaustralia.gov.au/raising-kids

Council of Single Mothers and Their Children: www.csmc.org.au

Parents Beyond Breakup: parentsbeyondbreakup.com

Solo Mums by Choice: www.smcaustralia.org.au

First Light. For widowed parents: www.firstlight.org.au

New Zealand

New Zealand government child support: www.govt.nz/browse/family-and-whanau/separating-or-getting-divorced/child-support

Mums4Mums. Supporting new mums: www.mums4mums.org.nz

Birthright. Single-parent charity: www.birthright.org.nz

Acknowledgements

From us both:
An enormous thank-you from both of us to our brilliant agent Kate Evans at PFD, for just getting this book from the start, and for 'getting' us too. Here's to many more mile-a-minute meetings and idea jumbles. And thanks to our editor Jillian Young at Little, Brown – for never making us feel like first-timers (despite the obvious rooky-ness). The enthusiasm from both of you for this book has fuelled it, and your wisdom has elevated it. Thanks also to the whole team at Little, Brown: Jillian Stewart, Lucie, Jess and everyone else behind the scenes on subbing and design – thank you.

And a huge thank you to each and every one of our incredible contributors for your time and what you've added to this book. To Helen, Natalie, Holly, Aaron, Ruth, James, Bethie, Jamie, Linton and Leon, the single- and solo-parent stories and experiences you've shared have inspired us to keep doing better. And our experts who have added so much to this book, thank you Charlotte, Kate, Layla, Natalye-Marrie, and the teams at Gingerbread, OnlyMums & Dads and Working Families.

From Zoë:
Rebecca, I am so glad that Frolo brought us together. I respect

and admire you so much, for many reasons. Thank you for your incredible way with words and for getting this important message out there to the world with me. I am so proud of us.

To my family – Mum, Dad, Brett, Ross and Dery – thank you for your support and love, and for understanding that I have needed to carve my own path. To the amazing Marilou: you are more than Billy's nanny, you are part of our family. I don't know how I would do any of it without your support.

To the Frolo Community for continuing to prove to me every day that magic exists, and that human kindness and connection trumps everything, and has the ability to change and save lives. You saved me. To the close friends I have made through Frolo: I honestly can't imagine my and Billy's world without you. And to my amazing non-single-parent friends who are so inclusive and supportive, and have never made me feel like a single parent: I hope you know who you are. Nikki Lannen, my fellow female tech founder: thank you for being a constant source of support over the last few years. You inspire me every day.

To anyone who has ever believed in me, and helped me believe in myself. There's no way I would have got to this point without you.

Thank you to Billy's dad Chris, for being the reason Billy is here. I hope we can always strive to put Billy first and focus on being the best co-parents possible for Billy.

And, Billy, thank you for making me want to do my very best and make you proud.

From Rebecca:
Thank you, Zoë, for not only building the Frolo Community and making single parents everywhere (including myself) feel less alone, but for collaborating on this book with me: our first co-parenting endeavour and we've birthed a beauty!

To every reader of my work who has ever taken the time to message me and tell me my words have helped you: this book is for you, because you made me believe it was needed.

Thank you to Jackie, my own single mum, who taught me that it doesn't take two parents at home to fill a house with love. And my late grandad, Ray, for showing me that father figures can be found outside the home (and in my heart, for ever). Thank you also to the rest of my family, made up of gloriously colourful 'halves' and 'steps' and 'exes' and 'in-laws'. I love you all. Thank you, Holly, for showing up for me when I needed you.

To Lucy and Jeremy at *Country & Town House*: you let me work flexibly before it was trendy. Thank you for putting your trust in me and providing me with a working set-up that has allowed me (and Jack) to thrive. Thank you to Grace, for listening to me talk about this book for a year of school runs, and helping out with Jack so regularly. Thank you to Nina, to whom I'm probably currently on the phone, without you I would go mad (or rather, madder), and Jessica, who listens and listens. I love you both.

Thank you to Jack's grandma (yes, Mum, you again) and granny (Lynette), for loving him so dearly and for all the childcare you provide so that I can make this single-mum thing work. And to Adam, for being the only person on earth who loves Jack as fiercely as I do. I know this isn't how you pictured raising children either, but we're getting better at this co-parenting thing, and our little boy is so happy.

You are happy, aren't you, Jack? It's infectious. Thank you for sharing it with me every day. I love you so very much. Thank you, thank you.

Index